Commerce as Politics

The Human Economy
Series editors:
Keith Hart, Goldsmiths, University of London
Theodoros Rakopoulos, University of Oslo

Those social sciences and humanities concerned with the economy have lost the confidence to challenge the sophistication and public dominance of the field of economics. We need to give a new emphasis and direction to the economic arrangements that people already share, while recognising that humanity urgently needs new ways of organising life on the planet. This series examines how human interests are expressed in our unequal world through concrete economic activities and aspirations.

Volume 8
Commerce as Politics: The Two Centuries of Struggle for Basotho Economic Independence
Sean M. Maliehe

Volume 7
Credit and Debt in an Unequal Society: Establishing a Consumer Credit Market in South Africa
Jürgen Schraten

Volume 6
Money at the Margins: Global Perspectives on Technology, Financial Inclusion and Design
Edited by Bill Maurer, Smoki Musaraj and Ivan V. Small

Volume 5
Money in a Human Economy
Edited by Keith Hart

Volume 4
From Clans to Co-ops: Confiscated Mafia Land in Sicily
Theodoros Rakopoulos

Volume 3
Gypsy Economy: Romani Livelihoods and Notions of Worth in the 21st Century
Edited by Micol Brazzabeni, Manuela Ivone Cunha and Martin Fotta

Volume 2
Economy for and against Democracy
Edited by Keith Hart

Volume 1
People, Money and Power in the Economic Crisis: Perspectives from the Global South
Edited by Keith Hart and John Sharp

Commerce as Politics

The Two Centuries of Struggle for Basotho Economic Independence

Sean M. Maliehe

berghahn
NEW YORK • OXFORD
www.berghahnbooks.com

First published in 2021 by
Berghahn Books
www.berghahnbooks.com

Library of Congress Cataloging-in-Publication Data

Names: Maliehe, Sean Morenakemang, author.
Title: Commerce as politics : the two centuries of struggle for Basotho economic independence / Sean M. Maliehe.
Other titles: Human economy ; v. 8.
Description: New York : Berghahn Books, 2021. | Series: The human economy; volume 8 | Includes bibliographical references and index.
Identifiers: LCCN 2020041627 (print) | LCCN 2020041628 (ebook) | ISBN 9781789209815 (hardback) | ISBN 9781789209822 (ebook)
Subjects: LCSH: Sotho (African people)–Economic conditions–19th century. | Sotho (African people)–Economic conditions–20th century. | Lesotho–Economic conditions. | Lesotho–Politics and government.
Classification: LCC HC920 .M34 2021 (print) | LCC HC920 (ebook) | DDC 338.96883–dc23
LC record available at https://lccn.loc.gov/2020041627
LC ebook record available at https://lccn.loc.gov/2020041628

British Library Cataloguing in Publication Data

A catalogue record for this book is available from the British Library

ISBN 978-1-78920-981-5 hardback
ISBN 978-1-78920-982-2 ebook

Emergent world society is the new human universal – not an idea, but the fact of our shared occupation of the planet crying out for new principles of association.

—Keith Hart, Jean-Louis Laville and Antonio David Cattani, 'Building the Human Economy Together'

An artist's duty as far as I'm concerned is to reflect the times … I choose to reflect the times and the situations in which I find myself. That to me is my duty. At this crucial time in our lives when everything is so desperate, when every day is a matter of survival, I don't think you can help but be involved.

Young people – black or white – know this. That's why they are so involved in politics. We will shape and mould this country. I will not be shaped and moulded by it anymore.

—Nina Simone, American singer and human rights activist

Contents

Acknowledgements

This book is based on my work on Lesotho: my BA Development Studies research project on the arrival and impact of Chinese traders in Lesotho; my BA History research project on the environmental factors in the rise and fall of the precolonial Basotho nation; my MA project on the emergence of colonial commerce (1870–1970); my PhD thesis on the history of commerce after national independence (1966–2012); and a book chapter on precolonial and nineteenth-century economic history Lesotho (1830s–1930s) published in Keith Hart (ed). 2017. *Money in the Human Economy*. New York: Berghahn Books.

The road to completion of this body of work and book was long and difficult. I owe my gratitude to the senior scholars who played a significant role in shaping my academic path. The idea that I could even produce a book came from Prof. Keith Hart. He assiduously worked with me in bringing this work to publication through the Human Economy book series at Berghahn Books. I am forever indebted to him. Upon completion of my PhD at the University of Pretoria, I was offered a three-year postdoctoral fellowship in the Human Economy Programme (2016–2018), and he advised me to work on my manuscript and begin new research on the development of mobile money in southern Africa (in Lesotho and Diepsloot, South Africa). Professors Hart and John Sharp co-founded and directed the Human Economy Programme in the Centre for the Advancement of Scholarship, funded by the Andrew W. Mellon Foundation and the University of Pretoria. I am grateful for the support I received through the Programme and colleagues, mostly PhD students and postdoctoral fellows, several of whom I continue to work with.

My gratitude also goes to my BA, MA and PhD supervisors: Ms Puleng Adams, Prof. Tefetso Mothibe, Prof. Motlatsi Thabane and Prof. Alois Mlambo. I appreciate their guidance highly. This is also an apology for the stress I caused them in my journey of learning. I could not finish this manuscript within the duration of my Pretoria research fellowship. In January 2019, I joined the 'Making of Modern Southern Africa' project led by Prof. Thula Simpson (Department of Historical and Heritage Studies, University of Pretoria). Prof. Simpson accorded me time and resources to complete this manuscript. My sincere gratitude goes to him also, and to Prof. Karren Harris, the Head of Department. I am grateful to the scholars that reviewed this manuscript. I would like to acknowledge *HISTORIA* and *African Economic History* for granting me the permission to reproduce some of the material I published with them.

I thank all the people I spoke to in the production of this work, as well as various information centres, organisations and associations. My special thanks go to the Lesotho Chamber of Commerce and Industry (LCCI). I thank Mr S. K. Phafane, Mr F. Hakane and Mr N. Seboka for granting me the opportunity to use LCCI as a platform to chronicle the economic history of contemporary Lesotho. I am also grateful for encouragement and support from my former teachers, particularly Dr Munyaradzi Mushonga, Dr Tumelo Tsikoane, Prof. Jesmuel Mataga, Mr Khotso Ketsi and Prof. Resetselemang Leduka.

My warmest thanks go to my friends and siblings for their contributions and support: J. Aerni-Flessner, J. Thumbran, E. Makhetha, S. Molapo, J. Schraten, T. Nyamunda, A. Young, B. Bae, N. Mbem, C. Makhalemele, F. Maunganidze, M. Lebona, L. Hlehlisi, M. Motšoehli, N. Ndweni, P. Sekamotho, Motlatsi, `Mabataung, Tebello, `Maleseli, Lekhanya, Teboho, Mpho, Naleli, Bohlokoa and Nala.

This book is dedicated to my parents and my son – Bataung, Motebang; 'Matebello, 'Maleseli; and Bokang Maliehe. My parents' history transcending repressive racial, cultural, economic and political borders is a beacon for my intellectual journey, and a constant reminder that humans can shape the world differently.

Like many Basotho men, my father worked in the South African mines. In the mid-1970s he took his father's position at the Western Areas Gold Mine, Gauteng. My mother's family owned businesses in this area. My maternal grandparents were originally from the Portuguese island of Madeira.

My parents' encounter defied apartheid laws prohibiting interracial relationships. They eloped to Lesotho in the mid-1980s, barely avoiding capture by apartheid authorities. It was only after the release of Nelson Mandela that my mother could return to South Africa. They remain happily married and true to their calling as African healers in Lesotho.

Like all grandparents in a labour-migration society, they take care of my son while I chase life and an intellectual journey. The one thing they taught us that matters is to emancipate ourselves, to carve our own space in the world and develop a sense of obligation to humanity.

Chronology

1500s	Sotho groups settle in the High Veld (Mohokare Valley)
1800s	Mfecane/Lifaqane wars
1820	Moshoeshoe moves from Menkhoaneng to Botha-Bothe Mountain
1824	Moshoeshoe moves from Botha-Bothe to Thaba-Bosiu Mountain
1833	Arrival of the Paris Evangelical Missionary Society
1836	First group of Boers/Afrikaners settles in the High Veld
1851	First Basotho–British War
1852	Second Basotho–British War
1858	First Basotho–Boer War
1862	Arrival of the Roman Catholic Missionaries
1865	Second Basotho–Boer War
1868	Third Basotho–Boer War
1868	Moshoeshoe's territory becomes a British Protectorate
1870	Moshoeshoe dies
1871	Imposition of colonial rule
1876	Arrival of the Anglican Church
1879	`Moorosi rebellion
1884	Third Basotho–British War (Gun War)
1890	Formation of the Basutoland Chamber of Commerce
1895	Arrival of Indian traders
1905	Formation of the National Council
1907	Formation of the Basutoland Progressive Association

1910	Integration into the Southern African Customs Union
1919	Formation of the League of Commoners
1925	Formation of the League of Justice
1931	Native Recruitment Corporation opens a branch in Basutoland
1940c	Formation of the Basuto Traders Association
1952	Formation of the Basutoland African Congress
1957	Formation of the Basutoland National Party
1966	Basotho gain independence from Britain
1967	Establishment of the Lesotho National Development Corporation
1968	Basotho traders form Mokhatlo oa Bahoebi Lesotho
1869	Basotho traders establish a bulk buying co-operative (Thekommoho)
1970	Declaration of the State of Emergency
1974	Basotho Congress Party leaders go into exile
1975	Establishment of the Basotho Enterprises Development Corporation
1976	Formation of the Lesotho Chamber of Commerce and Industry
1986	Military coup
1987	Lesotho implements Structural Adjustment Programmes
1993	Lesotho transitions to multiparty elections
1997	Formation of the Lesotho Congress for Democracy
1998	Military intervention by the Southern African Development Community
2000s	Influx of Fujianese traders
2005	Establishment of the Smart Partnership Hub
2005	Formation of the Mohloli Chamber of Business
2009	Formation of the Private Sector Foundation

2009	Establishment of the Business Council
2011	Basotho established the Coalition of Concerned Citizens
2012	End of Prime Minister Pakalitha Mosisili's fifteen-year rule
2012	First coalition government formed
2015	Second coalition government formed
2017	Third coalition government formed

Map 0.1. The Kingdom of Lesotho. *Source:* Library of Congress.

Introduction

In Lesotho,[1] commerce has a strong political dimension. To Basotho,[2] money and markets are a means of emancipation from authoritative rulers and exclusive formations. Along with technology, commerce facilitates a democratic aspiration for inclusion and social extension. Taking advantage of the two, Basotho have reached out, persistently and over time, to the world beyond their locality for economic advancement and political autonomy. Under conditions of poverty, repression and violence, a two-century-long Basotho struggle for economic independence lives on.

From the first to the last quarter of the nineteenth century, the Basotho under Moshoeshoe generated remarkable economic expansion at the leading edge of the Southern African region. They harnessed the potential of commerce and technology to establish a precarious independence under conditions of war, starvation and land loss. Escaping British rule in the Cape, Afrikaner groups occupied the interior of the region, conquering Basotho lands from the 1830s and 1840s. Until the 1860s, conflicts over land between the Basotho and Afrikaner groups were in full swing. They went to war over land three times: in 1858, 1865 and 1868, leading to British intervention. When the British annexed what was left of their territory in 1868, the Basotho had lost almost 80 per cent of it to the Afrikaners. The same year, diamonds were discovered in Kimberly, and gold in the Witwatersrand in 1886.

The British changed their approach. They now used political means and big capital to dismantle Basotho economic independence, so that the Basotho's only resource was to supply cheap labour for the mines in South Africa. Political aggression escalated throughout Southern Africa. The Basotho resisted this assault on their independence and went to war against the British in the Gun War of 1880–81. They emerged victorious but chose to align with the British for protection against the Afrikaners across the new border. The Basotho were sold out by the chiefs, who were roped into the colonial power matrix and were used in the colonial style to enforce 'indirect rule'. The system used taxes as one of the primary means to extract labour. In return for various benefits and privileges, the chiefs from then on primarily served colonial interests.

With the routinisation of labour migration, commerce – retail and wholesale – emerged as the pillar of the domestic economy; however, it was dominated by European traders who excluded both Basotho and, more recently, Indians. European traders combined with the colonial administration to use bureaucracy, legal apparatus and political influence to marginalise the two groups. The colonial system used rigid bureaucracy and big capital to dismantle Basotho precolonial economic formations.

In 1871, the colonial government passed the Mercantile Law. This was the first step towards formalising and regulating trade under colonial rule. The new laws were enforced in 1884, after the Gun War. This systematically undermined the independent trading formations and conditions that the Basotho had built for themselves after the Mfecane/Lifaqane wars – a series of regional cataclysms in the early 1800s. It now became compulsory to acquire a trading licence to open specific business premises. Their trading activities were informalised, vilified and criminalised. The colonial administration and British traders worked together to exclude others, and the Europeans' Basutoland Chamber of Commerce contributed significantly towards that end.

Against these restrictive measures, it took a protracted struggle for Basotho to gain access to local commerce. As a result, from the beginning of the twentieth century they formed political and business organisations to fight for inclusion and reformation of commerce. Their organisations were the Basutoland Progressive Association (1906), the League of Commoners (1919), the League of Justice (1925) and the Basotho Traders Association (1940c). With varying degrees of efficiency and ideology, they launched the twentieth-century liberation struggle. From the 1950s, political parties took over the independence movement.

To mask their repressive behaviour, the British administration and European traders held that politics had nothing to do with business, and often stigmatised the Basotho as 'a people with no business culture'. They were supposed to lack modern business acumen, an ethic of buying cheap and selling dear (*homo economicus*) and the spirit of entrepreneurship allegedly found in the West (Weber 1961; Schumpeter 1939). This attitude persists in modern Lesotho, with governments granting foreign traders privileges that they deny to their own citizens.

The period since 1966, when Lesotho gained independence from Britain, has matched that earlier phase of defeat without the buoyancy that preceded it in the nineteenth century. From 1966, Lesotho was ruled by the Basotho National Party. From 1970, the government turned to dictatorship, until it was overthrown by the military in 1986. In its own way, the shift from military rule to democracy since 1993 has resembled colonisation. The British laid down a rigid administration to secure labour migration to the South African mines, as we have seen. Postcolonial governments have used a version of this system to suppress Basotho commerce while relying on foreign economic interests and feeding their own local elites. One aim of this book is to show the similarities and differences between colonial empire and neocolonialism.

Optimistic of economic opportunities that would come with national independence, Basotho traders resuscitated the Basotho Traders Association in 1968. They formed a bulk-buying co-operative (Thekommoho) a year later to counter the European traders' monopoly and exclusive banking conditions. Basotho economic success, however, threatened cordial relations between the National Party and European traders. The majority of Basotho traders were leaders and influential members of the major opposition party, the Basotho Congress Party.

In 1970, the National Party lost elections to the Congress Party. In reprisal, Prime Minister Leabua Jonathan declared a State of Emergency, suspended the constitution and violently harassed the opposition. He destroyed the co-operative and Basotho economic solidarity. Opposition members were imprisoned or exiled after a failed uprising in 1974; in exile, they formed the Lesotho Liberation Army to destabilise the civilian dictatorship in an attempt to overthrow it.

Leabua was finally toppled by the military in the mid-1980s. South Africa had closed its borders with Lesotho; by then, Lesotho and South Africa's relations had reached their lowest ebb. From the mid-1950s, South Africa had earmarked Lesotho as a country to meet its pressing water demands, particularly in the industrial and mining hub of the 'Pretoria-Witswaterands-Vereeniging Complex'. Into the mid-1980s, the two countries had persistently disagreed on various conditionalities of the project. Meanwhile, water demands continued to escalate.

In January 1986, South Africa closed its borders with Lesotho in reprisal. It used as pretext an allegation that its neighbour was harbouring the African National Congress's Umkhonto we Size combatants. Lesotho imports almost 90 per cent of its manufactured goods and fuel from South Africa. Soon, the country was not able to replenish its stocks. With pressure building, the military surrounded the government complex, drove the civil servants out and took the Prime Minister hostage. Thereafter, a delegation led by Major General Justin M. Lekhanya took it upon itself to pay Pretoria a visit. Their mission was to request that South Africa lift the blockade, but the latter refused. Upon their return, the delegation announced via the national radio station (Radio Lesotho) that they had taken over government. The blockade was immediately lifted. Nine months later, Lesotho signed the water treaty and adopted the International Monetary Fund (IMF) and World Bank's Structural Adjustment Programmes.

The military dictatorship had scant regard for human rights. Conflicts within the government persisted, giving the impression that dictatorship held back the country, and the international community and the Southern African Development Community (SADC) pushed for the restoration of constitutional rule. In the late 1980s, exiled opposition members returned, and after the 1993 elections, the Congress Party finally ascended to power. The role of the people was significant in this transition.

Between 1996 and 1998, the government built the 'Manthabiseng Convention Centre on the Main South 1 Road, in the outskirts of the capital, Maseru. In April 1999, the government officially opened the new building, which was built with assistance from the People's Republic of China. Before it was built, a buzzing bus stop with shops and informal traders populated the area. The Centre commemorates the death of 'Manthabiseng Senatsi, a 56-year-old Mosotho woman. On 20 May 1991, a security guard working for a South African-owned business, Harties, assaulted and killed her. The guard had accused her of shoplifting after a baby she had on her back picked up a T-shirt (Tangri 1993).

There is more to this incident. Looking closely at the actions of the security guard, it is impossible to miss the scary amount of arbitrary power that these guards possessed, and the superiority they felt in carrying out an unjustifiable punishment. It is not farfetched to liken him to a 'house negro',[3] controlling the other slaves on a United States plantation. The security guard's actions were typical of the repressive power relations and despotic hierarchies that became normal in Basotho society following the imposition of colonial rule from the 1870s.

'Manthabiseng's death provoked violent attacks on foreign traders: especially Chinese and Indians, whom, people felt, the government was protecting at their expense. As we have seen, Europeans traders enjoyed such privileges. About 35 people were killed and 63 were badly injured; 77 enterprises were looted and damaged while 16 were burnt down. 13 of 60 foreign-owned businesses were shut down as their owners fled to South Africa, together with many expatriates (Tangri 1993). This remains the most violent episode against foreigners in Lesotho.

That day, the school bus driver came rushing into our classroom to take us home. With my brother and sister, I attended the Seventh Day Adventist Primary School located about 800 m from the centre of the upheavals. We could hear glass smashing, stones banging and people screaming as we navigated through the midst of the havoc. Hiding below the backseat, we were petrified. Basotho indiscriminately called the Indians, Chinese, and anyone like them 'coolies' and 'mulattos'. We fell in this category, as we mixed Basotho and Portuguese ancestries.

After 1993, the Congress Party leader, Ntsu Mokhehle, ruled until 1998. His protégé, Pakalitha Mosisili, succeeded him, ruling for the next decade and a half under a new party, the Lesotho Congress for Democracy. To address the country's economic challenges, the government relied on the newly introduced market policies. It adopted privatisation policies to pare back the role of the state in the economy. The 'self-regulating market' or 'free market' model of capitalism was thus given priority.

Accordingly, the government privatised various state-owned companies. In his popular economic plea, Prime Minister Mosisili persuaded Basotho to '… work together to create many Basotho millionaires because they [would] create jobs for other Basotho and help in curbing unemployment and poverty'.[4] In its pursuits, the government prioritised the interests of elites and foreign investors. They neglected and marginalised the majority of the people in the economy. Mosisili's reign became authoritarian, as well; he was dethroned through a coalition of three opposition parties in 2012, following the 'Mother of All Protests' in 2011 – the biggest solidarity movement in contemporary Lesotho.

Owing to authoritarianism, corruption and elitism, the Congress disintegrated from 1993 on the one hand, producing multiple offspring. On the other hand, waves of popular unrest characterised the 2000s, as people protested through their trade unions and associations. In the early 2010s, they formed the 'Coalition of Concerned Citizens', and in August 2011, they marched in defence of the social fabric in the context of ruinous market policies. The major opposition party at the time – the All-Basotho Convention – became the people's viable option; however, it did not have a majority. As a result, it went into a coalition with two parties to govern: the Lesotho Congress for Democracy and the Basotho National Party. From June 2012, Thomas Thabane was the Prime Minister.

Amid this euphoria, I was immersed in my doctoral research in 2013. I was studying the history of Basotho in local commerce in the period between 1966 and 2012 – the postcolonial period – while based at the Lesotho Chamber of Commerce and Industry (LCCI). The Chamber helped organise my ethnographic explorations. I travelled around the ten districts of the country, collecting oral histories of Basotho business owners. I continued to dig for the past in the archives. This was a continuation of my masters' research on the emergence of colonial commerce and Basotho participation between the 1870s and 1970s (Maliehe 2011; 2015).

In one of my expeditions, I attended a 'market expo' in Maseru. The new government had organised this business promotion event on the football pitch of the Maseru Club, a few metres away from the Chamber headquarters. Negotiating my way through a buzzing crowd, I entered a section of the open fields, teeming with young Basotho entrepreneurs. Their commodities were neatly packed on tables; some hung on strings from their tiny stalls. They sold artistic African clothes, printed T-shirts and hats, hand-made jewellery and shoes, paintings, food and similar items. Navigating a maze of stands, my fascination temporarily trumped my curiosity as a researcher.

I submerged myself in conversations with old friends, acquaintances and strangers, using our mother tongue, Sesotho. Hope and despair melted together in smiles and melancholy when we spoke of the hardships of Basotho entrepreneurs under the present repressive conditions. After high school and college, many never obtained formal jobs in government, non-governmental organisations (NGOs) or private corporations. The mines in South Africa were no longer hiring young men. Many still worked in South Africa as informal workers and traders or artisanal diamond and gold diggers in closed mining shafts.

Closer to the podium at the centre, bigger stalls were occupied by HIV/AIDS organisations and other NGOs, government departments, insurance companies, banks and mobile network operators. I met old friends from the National University of Lesotho – for a time the only university in the country. Some had become senior officials and middle managers. In smart-casual attire, they were flamboyantly dressed for an informal Friday event. Each had two mobile phones in their hands: a smartphone and a cheap basic phone. I was one of them.

With my scholarship at the University of Pretoria's Human Economy Programme, my income could be matched only by a husband and wife's combined salaries working in Lesotho's civil service. My monthly rent in Pretoria would have supported an urban household in Lesotho. I was one of few Basotho who broke into prestigious fellowships abroad. I could return to a university teaching position at home or seek greener pastures further afield. The entrepreneurs I met that day from around the country managed precarity only by meeting the stringent conditions of the banks. Good behaviour and prudent economic decisions kept them afloat. Informal saving clubs (*stokvels*) are in many ways more reliable.

I moved closer to the centre of the exhibition. Here, the crowd was being entertained by local poets, comedians, 'house-music' DJs and players on a podium decorated with flyers and towering speakers. Young photographers competed to capture things, moments and people. Official reports of the event had to match the colour of social media updates. Soliciting views, local reporters took chosen participants to quieter corners of the fields.

Now that I was closer to the platform, my attention was captured by the Master of Ceremonies, who called to the stage an enthusiastic group of Vodacom staff. Their leader took the microphone and spoke of a new mobile money: M-Pesa. I felt that I was studying the past, so I made little of it then. I soon went back to Pretoria, returning in 2015 upon my completion. After returning to Pretoria, as a member of the Chamber and former business owner, I stayed in contact with Lesotho's business community.

Before long the landscape had changed significantly. Mobile money transformed Southern Africa's local economies, blending various actors – big and small – in a new financial ecosystem. I now studied the emergence of mobile money in Lesotho and South Africa; my ethnographic site was the informal township of Diepsloot, north of Johannesburg. In 2017, the United Nations Development Programme and Central Bank of Lesotho commissioned me to explore mobile technologies and financial innovations among poor and rural communities in Lesotho.

A sense that the country was finally on a new development path was quickly shrouded by political conflicts and instability. In the five years following 2012, Lesotho held three snap elections, amid widespread violence, political instability, mismanagement of national resources and economic stagnation. Between 2012 and 2015, three parties formed government; seven between 2015 and 2017; and four up to 2020. The coalition government led by Thabane served for two years, from 2012 to 2014. In attempts to undermine the opposition, Prime Minister Thabane embarked on a massive anti-corruption campaign, which threatened various key figures from the previous government. In reprisal and for their own preservation, the opposition parties destabilised the government, until Thabane and his associates were exiled to South Africa in 2014. In 2015, elections were held in their absence. A new coalition government of seven political parties, led by the Democratic Congress, was formed.

The cabinet was increased from thirteen to twenty-three members to accommodate party elites. Conflicts persisted. Following the murder of the military commander, Lieutenant-General Maaparankoe Mahao, South Africa and subsequently the Southern African Development Community (SADC) intervened at the invitation of the government. (In many respects, South Africa and the SADC's interventions resembled mid-nineteenth-century British mediation). Thereafter, in 2017, Lesotho held its third election in five years. Exiled party leaders returned. Prime Minister Thabane regained his position as ruler in partnership with three other parties.

As before, the people had placed their hopes in the leadership of the Prime Minister. He had emerged as the 'liberator' of the people against Congress despotism. To the people's disappointment, he swung in the opposite direction. First, he delayed implementing security reforms and other recommendations of the SADC. Second, he turned against the mandate of ending corruption, working for the people and reviving the economy. Like his predecessors, he misused his power and squandered national resources among close associates.

Lastly and most controversially, the Prime Minister, in his eighties, married a third wife in her early forties. The First Lady – 'the Grace Mugabe of Lesotho' – was criticised for meddling heavily in party and government affairs, causing a division in the former and instigating the dismissal of some cabinet members. Between January and February 2020, the two were in front of the Magistrate Court, answering charges related to the assassination of the Prime Minister's second wife (being a contender for the position of First Lady, she was gunned to death a day before Thabane's inauguration in June 2017). Apprehensive of another spree of violence, South Africa intervened yet again, with its Minister of Finance, Tito Mboweni, subsequently making the historically controversial call that Lesotho must become part of South Africa (Burke 2020).

The country's political and economic conditions continue to deteriorate. Lesotho still depends on external forces beyond its control – the Southern African Customs Union (SACU), foreign aid, South Africa and foreign direct investment. As demonstrated by the 'market expo' episode discussed above, a new economy is emerging, and there are historical antecedents for it; this is not the first time that the Basotho have used technology, money and markets to shape their own future. The main aim of this book is to revisit the economic history of the Basotho in order to drawn lessons from their past. In a world where only 'expert knowledge' yielded by economics already rules supreme, we cannot ignore the roles of the people and their history in making and remaking their economic lives.

It has become commonplace to ascribe African underdevelopment to postcolonial failure to make a decisive break with imperialism. But monolithic fatalism of this kind misses much from economic history that might support a different view of what is now possible for countries like Lesotho. A more promising economic future can be envisaged, drawing on a more nuanced vision of history. I argue in this book that the Basotho have repeatedly asserted their own economic agency in the last two centuries.

We need to understand the dialectical relationship between this small part of the Southern African region and the changing nature of the global forces confronting it. In Lesotho's case, South Africa is key. The inverse is also true: without Lesotho, South Africa could neither meet its labour demands in the mines before, nor its desperate water needs today. The Basotho's ability to negotiate unrestricted movement between these two territories shaped their variable fortunes, between general success (in the precolonial period, 1820s–70s), limited resistance to repression (in the colonial period, 1870–1960s) and general failure (in the postcolonial period, since 1966). A comparative analysis of these three phases frames the organisation of this book.

With differing means and degrees of efficiency, the Basotho have had to defend themselves against unfavourable local and regional conditions across time. Unlike many African communities in the region, however, they maintained their sovereignty at first, against heavy odds. Transcending differences in race, ideology and religion, they formed alliances based on mutual interests. Throughout their economic history, Basotho struggles for economic independence have had money and markets at their centre. The Basotho attempted to harness the emancipatory potential of both. Commerce always had a strong political dimension; it reinforced an economic interdependence that instilled in Lesotho and South Africa recognition that they needed each other. Both countries benefited from this reciprocal relationship.

In many respects, both the Basotho's loss of their lands and colonialism later in the nineteenth century were instrumental in the destruction of this relationship. On the one hand, the Afrikaners conquered about 80 per cent of the Basotho's productive lands. Lesotho remained, but as a tiny mountainous shell of its former, larger, more agriculturally productive self. In the context of increasing population, the ramifications were dire. On the other hand, the British used political means and big capital to dismantle Basotho economic independence from the last quarter of the nineteenth century. European traders (and now Chinese traders) dominated local commerce to the exclusion of the Basotho, who had to fight for inclusion and reformation of commerce.

The twentieth-century mining complex has now collapsed. Conditions are desperate. Despite inherent hierarchies, the primary mission for the Basotho now is to rediscover a more equal relationship with South

Africa. As in the nineteenth century, technology now provides a global dimension to the development problem and offers new possibilities for economic revival. These possibilities must of course be inclusive and prioritise the people. Not uniquely in the region, the Basotho have still not achieved a society based even remotely on social justice.

The means of building something like this is economic democracy. Technology, markets and money are intrinsic to such a project, even if they have often been engines of inequality. The human economy approach is one way of putting local people first in the global context of general human interests (Hart et al. 2010; Hart and Sharp 2014; Hart 2015, 2017). Against tremendous odds over two centuries, the Basotho have struggled for a fair share of their country's commerce. This political struggle provides a thread that links the country's present dilemmas to its past and future. For this reason, this book looks back to the times and spaces in which the Basotho have brought about economic success, in order to rethink how a future may be built to bring about a more just Lesotho for all of its residents.

Organisation of the Book

Part I chronicles the rise and fall of the precolonial Basotho nation (1820s–70s), encompassing Chapters 1 and 2. Part II explores the rise of colonial commerce and the economic dimensions of the liberation struggles (1870s–1966). It has three Chapters: 3, 4 and 5. Part III deals with the period since 1966. With five Chapters (6, 7, 8, 9 and the Conclusion), it is roughly equal in size to the first two parts. Part III is largely an account of the postcolonial counter-revolution against the movement for independence.

Chapter 1 shows that ordinary Basotho allied with Christian missionaries in adopting new agricultural technologies to trade in regional markets. Others worked in the colonies to build their wealth in a domestic economy dominated by the chiefs. These two streams introduced to the Basotho and the region the transformative power of horses and guns. As a result, the Basotho became significant actors in the making of a new regional economy by the mid-nineteenth century.

We see in Chapter 2 that the rise and expansion of Basotho economic power was halted by the Afrikaners' conquest of the most fertile of Lesotho's lands. This led to British intervention and annexation in 1868. On the heels of the discovery of minerals in South Africa, the British came to view Lesotho as a labour reserve. As with other communities in the region, the British resorted to political aggression. The colonial administration used rigid bureaucracy and big capital to dismantle Basotho economic independence and to meet increasing labour demands in the mines. From this point on, Lesotho was integrated into the new mining complex as an unequal actor.

Chapter 3 (1870–1930s) explores the emergence of colonial commerce, retail and wholesale. It demonstrates how commerce replaced pre-colonial trading formations to become the main pillar of the local economy, which was dominated by European traders. The Europeans monopolised commerce at the exclusion of both the Basotho and Indian traders. Working closely with the colonial government, they protected only their interests. Their association, the Chamber of Commerce, was indispensable to their pursuits. Through political means and manipulation of colonial legislature, they controlled trade throughout the country.

Against these restrictive measures, it took a protracted struggle for Basotho to gain a foothold in local commerce. Chapter 4 (1900s–66) explores the challenges faced by, and survival strategies of, the first generation of Basotho commercial entrepreneurs. It demonstrates how partnerships amongst themselves and with Europeans and Indians formed part of their attempts to address their problems of access to credit and stock. Further, the chapter examines their breakthrough in the mid-1950s and the rise of the co-operative movement in commerce.

In Chapter 5 (still in the period 1900s–1966) I describe the antithesis to colonial empire, the twentieth-century liberation struggle. I focus here on Basotho political efforts aimed at the reformation of colonial commerce. Through their political and business organisations, the Basotho fought for inclusion in commerce as the struggle for self-rule intensified in the 1950s and 1960s. I argue here that these organisations articulated the political and economic hardships and aspirations of the Basotho. They collaborated with other African communities in South Africa; the Progressive Association focused on the Indigenous urban middle classes, while the League of Commoners and the League of Justice connected the urban areas to the rural masses. From the 1950s, political parties took over the movement, leading to national independence in 1966.

Chapter 6 explores Lesotho's experimentations with the state model for developing the national economy after 1966. Choosing to work with European traders rather than their own people, the government suppressed Basotho entrepreneurial initiatives. As previously discussed, the majority of Basotho traders were leaders and members of the major opposition party, the Basotho Congress Party. When the Congress Party was outlawed in the 1970s following Prime Minister Leabua Jonathan's coup, these entrepreneurs were in a precarious position. After the coup, the ruling National Party used development to expand despotism. The real casualty of this political crackdown was Basotho economic solidarity and democracy.

In Chapter 7, we examine the struggles of the Lesotho state in the 1980s, with the military toppling the civilian dictatorship. This government subsequently adopted the IMF and World Bank Structural Adjustment Programmes. These policies helped bring about flows of international capital for the construction of the Lesotho Highlands Water Project meant to supply water to South Africa. This was Lesotho's cue for a neoliberal turn that remains with us. The chapter demonstrates how South Africa took advantage of Lesotho's dependency to strong-arm it into signing the water treaty, and argues that the new market policies promoted elitism, patronage politics and corruption. Democracy and people's economic advancement initiatives were the victims, and the policies aggravated poverty and inequality.

Chapter 8 examines the rise of Basotho economic solidarity in defence of the social fabric, in a historic context of global neoliberal exclusion, patronage politics and economic stagnation. The chapter argues that through the 'Coalition of Concerned Citizens' solidarity movement, Basotho fought collectively for the democratisation of the economy. In this ongoing struggle, Basotho are demanding that the government make provision for their free movement across the border, and calling on the government to renew the agenda for the return of the 'Conquered Territories' from South Africa. In this way, Basotho have demonstrated awareness that their economic survival has always depended on how they navigated between Lesotho and South Africa.

If the Basotho had one hope for economic improvement after the collapse of the mining economy, it was in local commerce. The transition to democracy in 1993 and the coming to power of the Congress Party brought about a sense of optimism that Basotho-run businesses would finally have a chance to flourish. Chapter 9 chronicles the rise of Chinese traders in Lesotho, and how they quickly transformed rural Lesotho's trading economy, pushing out many Basotho traders. In a context of diminishing economic opportunities, Basotho reactions varied in political intensity and pragmatism. As before, they became politically expressive while they sought to reignite the co-operative movement to counter the Chinese monopoly.

It was in this context that mobile money developed. Mobile money widened Basotho business activities, enabling Basotho to act as agents in the new financial ecosystem. This chapter documents these two major developments in local commerce. Its main observation is that while we cannot predict the future, what is currently happening in Lesotho has its historical antecedents, which demonstrate that Basotho are capable of using technology and commerce to advance their economic interests in a competitive context.

In the conclusion, I reprise the main argument of the book. Summarising key features of the country's three epochs, I reflect on the relationship between commerce and politics. Across these phases, I demonstrate that commerce offered Basotho the means of emancipation from repressive rulers and formations. Under conditions of poverty, repression and violence, a two-century long Basotho struggle for economic independence continues. Reflecting on this economic history, I observe that the Basotho's economic pursuits and political autonomy are connected to how they forged a relationship of interdependence with South Africa in particular, despite inherent hierarchies.

In this chapter, I also reflect on how a human economy approach shaped my periodisation and interpretation of Basotho economic history. I place Basotho economic pursuits and interests at the centre of competing regional and global forces which date to the early nineteenth century, particularly after the Mfecane and Napoleonic Wars, when the British took over the Cape from Dutch. I demonstrate Basotho abilities to forge partnerships with those that supported their democratic aspirations, and I argue that this history has important lessons for the current Basotho generation with regards to shaping their economic future.

Furthermore, I align this narrative with the renewed interest in African economic history. In an intellectual landscape in which cliometrics – the reduction of economic history to econometrics – has powerful adherents, I argue that the refusal to acknowledge the politics in economics serves only ruling interests.

NOTES

1. The name Lesotho was made official in 1966 to refer to the territory known as Basutoland in the colonial era. In this study, Lesotho is used to refer to the territory throughout the precolonial and colonial periods, and I sometimes use the names interchangeably. Basutoland also appears in quotations, and I use it as a descriptive term for laws, institutions and so on.
2. In colonial orthography, 'Mosotho' (plural, 'Basotho') was spelled 'Musoto' (plural, 'Basuto'), and 'Lesotho' was 'Lesuto', though it was officially 'Basutoland'. Their dominant language, 'Sesotho', was written as 'Sesuto'. Minority African languages included Mphuthi, Xhosa and Ndebele.

3. The African American and Muslim activist Malcom X popularised the contrast between a 'field negro' and a 'house negro' in his famous 1963 speech, 'Message to the Grass Roots'. He advanced that a 'field negro' was subjected to harsh conditions outside while the 'house negro' enjoyed a comparatively better life in the master's house. That life, however, was subject to the conditions that they sustained existing power structures and reinforced exploitative relations in everyday life.
4. 'Mosisili's Rich Dream', *Lesotho Times*, 13 January 2010. Retrieved 11 August 2020 from http://lestimes.com/mosisilis-rich-dream/.

REFERENCES

Burke, J. 2020. 'Lesotho PM Requests Immunity from Charge of Murdering Wife', *The Guardian*, 24 February 2020. Retrieved 4 March 2020 from https://www.theguardian.com/world/2020/feb/24/lesotho-pm-thomas-thabane-surprise-court-appearance-over-wife-murder.

Hart, K. (ed.). 2015. *Economy for and against Democracy*. New York: Berghahn Books.

———. (ed.). 2017. *Money in a Human Economy*. New York: Berghahn Books.

Hart, K., and J. Sharp (eds). 2014. *People, Money and Power in the Economic Crisis: Perspectives from the Global South*. New York: Berghahn Books.

Hart, K., J. Laville and A.D. Cattani. 2010. 'Building the Human Economy Together', in K. Hart, J. Laville and A.D. Cattani (eds), *The Human Economy: A Citizen's Guide*. Cambridge: Polity Press, pp. 1–17.

Maliehe, S. 2011. 'Basotho Traders' Struggle for Access to, and Control over, Local Trade in Colonial and Immediate Postcolonial Lesotho, 1870–1970', MA dissertation. Roma: National University of Lesotho.

———. 2015. 'A History of Indigenously-Owned Business in Postcolonial Lesotho: Politics, Constraints, Marginalisation and Survival, 1966–2012', Ph.D. dissertation. Pretoria: University of Pretoria.

Schumpeter, J.A. 1939. *Business Cycles: A Theoretical, Historical and Statistical Analysis of the Capitalist Process*. London: McGraw-Hill Book Company.

Tangri, R. 1993. 'Foreign Business and Political Unrest in Lesotho', *African Affairs* 92(367): 223–38.

Weber, M. 1961. *General Economic History*. New York: Collier Books.

Part I

The Rise and Fall of the Basotho Nation

CHAPTER 1

The Formation of the Basotho Nation, 1820s–1870s

Introduction

The nineteenth century saw the making of modern southern Africa, including Lesotho. The Mfecane/Lifaqane wars were a turning point. The region experienced a series of prolonged and severe droughts in the first two decades of the nineteenth century, leading to military competition over resources and trade. These wholesale regional disruptions started on the eastern coast among the Zulu people of King Shaka. Under Moshoeshoe's leadership and influence, various Bantu-speaking communities and refugees that had been scattered over the region came to form the nucleus of the Basotho nation in the 1820s and 1830s (Eldredge 1993; Hamilton 1995; Omer-Cooper 1987; Thompson 1975; Sanders 1975).

This period coincided with European global expansion and Evangelical anti-slavery crusades. Due to contact with Europeans – missionaries, Afrikaners and the British – the nascent Basotho nation was integrated into the modern global economy after the Napoleonic wars, when the British took over the Cape from the Dutch. What began as a refreshment station on the Asian trade route dominated by the Dutch East India Company now changed the region's history. Its occupants settled and made permanent inroads into the interior from the 1830s and 1840s (Feinstein 2005; Swart 2010).

Upon Moshoeshoe's request, missionaries worked among the Basotho from the early 1830s. They promoted commerce, introduced new agricultural technologies and supported people's individual rights. As a result, two interconnected economic paths for ordinary Basotho emerged within a domestic economy that was dominated by the chiefs. One stream provided labour to the Europeans in the Cape and the Free State, while the other provided grain and livestock to various communities in the region.

These groups introduced horses and guns to the rest of the Basotho. The two technologies transformed trade, communication, transportation and war. By the 1850s, the Basotho were a significant part of the new regional trade networks connecting the interior with the coastal areas, and became the 'granary' for the new diamond-mining towns in South Africa by the 1870s. Murray, a pioneer of the 1980s school of political economy in southern Africa, focused on this latter period, with little attention given to the period that preceded it (1980, 1981). Murray chronicled the rise and fall of Basotho peasantry, rebutting neoclassical tropes that the Basotho lacked agrarian skills. Scholars that focused on the earlier period examined the political achievements of Moshoeshoe and land loss (Omer-Cooper 1987; Thompson 1975; Sanders 1975).

Covering the period between the 1820s and 1870s, this chapter examines the emergence of this new post-Mfecane regional economy. It demonstrates that the role of ordinary people was pertinent in Basotho expansion. Money and trade connected their territory to distant markets; the result was the creation of an interdependent formation based on mutual exchange of commodities and labour. The political and economic resilience of the Basotho was strengthened as well.

Moshoeshoe's Nation-Building Project

The consensus of historians and linguists is that Basotho farmers were the descendants of Bantu-speaking Iron Age communities from West Africa who had settled along the border of modern-day Nigeria and Cameroon. By 300 BC, some groups had migrated to the great lakes of East Africa, and had reached the east-African coast by the third century AD. Some made their way south by the fourth and fifth centuries, where they found San and Khoi-Khoi hunter-gatherers (Hamilton et al. 2012; Parsons 1993; Omer-Cooper 1987).

By the sixteenth century, the Sotho-speaking communities had moved deeper into the region's central and southwestern parts, while the Nguni-speaking communities settled on the southeast fringes along the coast. The northern Sotho groups, particularly the Tswana (Batswana), occupied the dry plains of the Kalahari (Kgalagadi), while the southern Sotho communities migrated into the southern Highveld, populating the area beyond the Lekoa and Mohokare Rivers (Parsons 1993; Omer-Cooper 1987). These groups were organised in small semi-autonomous chiefdoms, which expressed their identity through clan totems, *liboko* (Mothibe 2002a: 3–10).

The Iron Age communities depended on crop production and herding livestock. They supplemented these with hunting and collecting wild vegetables – male and female occupations respectively. They engaged in reciprocal economic exchanges within their groups and participated in long-distance trade with other communities in the region, such as the Nguni-speaking peoples of the east coast. They traded household utensils made from iron and copper, iron hoes, animal skins, cattle, tobacco and other goods (Eldredge 1993: 19–21).

Beads were used as a medium of exchange for long-distance trade. They could be given different values according to their colour. This was because beads were 'fungible, could not easily be obtained, and could be given different values according to their size and colours'. They were 'considered as money, to be employed only as a medium of trade with distant tribes and for the purchase of more expensive articles'. Additionally, the 'beads facilitated the relay trade system in which groups that traded directly with one another but did not need each other's goods accepted compensation in beads that could be used elsewhere to obtain the goods they did need' (Eldredge 1993: 21).

Within the Basotho groups, beads appear to have been introduced in the eighteenth century by Mohlomi, a regionally renowned senior chief, healer, philosopher, sage and traveller (Machobane 1990). Early beads were named after him as the 'beads of Mohlomi'. Oral tradition also recalls that beads were obtained through trade with communities on the eastern coast. When they were in short supply, a barter system facilitated exchanges. The AmaHlubi and the AmaZizi Nguni groups from the east coast 'crossed the mountains to trade with the BaKoena as early as the seventeenth century; bringing knives, spatulas, and hoes to exchange for animal skins, cattle, and tobacco' (Eldredge 1993: 21). These regional trade networks were disrupted by the Mfecane wars.

The Mfecane upheavals coincided with the rise to power of a junior chief of the Kuena (crocodile) clan of the Bamokoteli lineage known as Lepoqo – later, Moshoeshoe, a name he assumed following successful and celebrated cattle raiding adventures (Sanders 1975: 23). With these expeditions, Moshoeshoe's wealth and popularity grew. He was undoubtedly an impressive warrior, full of the youthful arrogance, ambition and aggression necessary for political success and adoration in a patriarchal and hyper-masculine society. The mentorship of Mohlomi moulded him into the wise leader that he became – a nation builder (Ellenberger 1912: 107).

After marrying, Moshoeshoe had to leave his father's village of Menkhoaneng to start his own – this was customary among the Sotho groups. In preparation, he gathered his age-mates and other clans. He welcomed many war refugees, providing them with food, shelter and security. He further co-opted and subordinated weaker neighbouring chiefdoms, and formed alliances with stronger ones. This is why the Basotho form a heterogeneous society today (Sanders 1975: 23).

In the search for a more defendable fortress, Moshoeshoe moved with his followers from Menkhoaneng to Botha-Bothe Mountain in 1820. When they arrived, they inhabited a vast cave on the southern side below the summit, and later built a village on the mountain top. The mountain had good pastures and strong perennial springs that supported their mixed-farming economy. Despite its fertile lands, rainfall and reliable streams, Botha-Bothe Mountain was not easily defendable, as it was connected to the Maloti mountain ranges on its southern side, making access by enemies possible (Walton 1959: 18).

Following a three-month siege by the Batlokoa clan, Moshoeshoe and his people were forced to leave Botha-Bothe Mountain. Their arch-rivals destroyed their crops in the fields and prevented their livestock from accessing pasture and water sources down the mountain (Thompson 1975: 41). Soon, Moshoeshoe's 'grain supplies were exhausted; they could no longer hunt … the proverbial *tlala ea bojalikata* [sic], the famine which reduces to gnawing old karosses, became a reality, and they killed their dogs and ate meat which they knew was rotten, for nothing was left' (Sanders 1975: 33).

During the siege, Moshoeshoe sent his messengers (intelligence gatherers, *lihloela*, and fast runners, *lititimi*) to Chief Sepheka, a contemporary Nguni chief and ally, to ask for his assistance. Sepheka came to their rescue and launched a surprise attack at night. During the battle, Moshoeshoe had a visit from a fellow kinsman who informed him of a place in the south that would make a better fortress. Moshoeshoe sent a delegation of messengers and intelligence gatherers to survey the proposed area. The delegation returned with an excellent report of a mesa they had found in the south. In the winter of 1824, Moshoeshoe and his people escaped to the new mountain fortress, which they subsequently named 'Thaba-Bosiu' ('the mountain of the night'). Fortified with traditional medicine, this meant that it grew at night to deceive adversaries (Ellenberger 1912: 145).

Thaba-Bosiu is a mesa in the valley of the Little Caledon (Phuthiatsana) River. A belt of steep sandstone cliffs encircles the summit. Detached from all neighbouring hills, it is in an amphitheatre of mountain ranges. These features made it possible for watchers to see enemies in all directions. A dolerite dyke cuts the sandstone cliffs in the northern side of the summit, providing seven defendable passes to the top. Moshoeshoe assigned his family members to set up their villages on the passes to guard them. The mountain had a big cave where Moshoeshoe's wives and other villagers hid during wars. The area around the mountain and its top boasted good pastures and arable lands to support mixed farming, and was well-watered, with about eight good perennial springs. The mountaintop plains were large enough to accommodate a good number of villages, especially for the royal family and other high-ranking families. At a short distance, a river meandered at the foot of the mountain slopes, providing water for the inhabitants and their animals (Walton 1959: 18).

During attacks, Moshoeshoe's strategy was to volley spears and roll an avalanche of stones down on climbing adversaries. This was the primary means of defence and a highly successful one. On the left of Moshoeshoe's village, there are the remains of a cairn. Visitors, as a gesture of respect to the chief, added a stone to the cairn on arrival. Ambrose argues that: '[N]o doubt the cairn was plundered for missiles in times of wars' (Ambrose n.d.: 13–14).

Between 1827 and 1865, eight major attacks failed. For example, in 1828 the AmaNgwane Nguni group attacked Moshoeshoe's fortress. Because of their superior numbers, they were on course to overwhelm the defenders. Their girls had already brought beer to celebrate the victory. However, fewer than five thousand Basotho warriors defeated them, led by Moshoeshoe's two eldest sons, Letsie and Molapo. In 1829, when Moshoeshoe had gone cattle raiding, the Batlokoa again attacked his people, but the old men and young boys who had been left to protect the summit passes defeated them. In 1831, the AmaNdebele of Mzilikazi (a breakaway Zulu group) attacked Thaba-Bosiu; like the others, they were repelled by avalanches of rocks down the mountain (Ambrose n.d.; Thompson 1975; Sanders 1975).

Moshoeshoe's acquisition of guns and horses played a crucial role in consolidating his supremacy in the region. Cattle occupied a central economic and symbolic position in Basotho society, but the horse was now elevated to a similar position, and it played a crucial role in social transformation. The horse increased military, communication and transport efficiency. As Swart (2010: 100) observes, 'The Basotho experienced the horse as a revolution in the military sense, a vital cog in the machinery of state formation'. They also 'operated as a cohesive cultural force, continuing to be central in sports, festivals, social relations (although secondary to cattle) and funeral rituals'. Swart observes further that:

> Key leaders like Mzilikazi, Sekonyela, Moshoeshoe, Dingane and Hintsa[1] all turned their attention to ensuring that their combatants were mounted and armed as far as possible. There were also initiatives from ordinary people themselves to acquire horses and guns. Gun and horse ownership seeped through to the Caledon Valley, Highveld and eastern seaboard (from the

> Cape). The acquisition happened rapidly: in 1800, for example, Tswana were on foot fighting off mounted raiders, but a generation later they themselves had access to guns and horses. Similarly, in the 1820s, Xhosa factions simply hungered after horses, but by 1846 they were able to mobilise as many as 7,000 armed mounted men. But only one African group became a wholly mounted polity – the Basotho. (Ibid.: 78–79)

Individuals working in the Cape under white and Griqua farmers were the first to carry the news of these two pieces of military weaponry back home. At first, they were acquired from the Cape and across the Orange River in exchange for labour, as spoils of border disputes with the Afrikaners in the early 1830s, and through raids. Moshoeshoe is said to have imported about two hundred horses between 1833 and 1838. By 1842, he had an army of some five hundred horsemen; a decade later, this had risen to six thousand soldiers, on horseback and adorned in European regalia (Swart 2010: 77–102).

By 1850, a British official observed that '[t]he Basuto people have within the last few years become exceedingly rich in cattle and horses', and that they possessed 'more firearms than all other tribes in the [Orange River] Sovereignty put together' (Swart 2010: 88). In 1875, thirty-five thousand horses were counted in Basutoland, and the figure had increased to over eighty thousand by 1891 (ibid.: 94–96).

Within the region, the Basotho became famous as the 'horse people' due to their success in breeding, training, riding and trading horses. They developed a breed which came to be known as the 'Basotho Pony'. The biophysical environment was crucial for its development; the mountainous topography and good pastures, in a relatively disease-free zone, aided in the development of a much-desired, hardy and 'all very square-built active' phenotype (Swart 2010: 98).

The Basotho breed was an adoption and adaption of the 'Cape Horse', a stock animal that developed in the seventeenth and eighteenth centuries. The Dutch East India Company commissioned a refreshment station in the Cape to feed the scurvy-ridden and malnourished crews of ships voyaging to the East Indies. This is how horses came to southern Africa. The Dutch settlers had the ambition to create a 'colony', and that needed horses, amongst other things. But the Company saw the Cape just as a 'refreshment station', and refused permission for a colony. The few horses imported from Holland often died of horse sickness in the new environment (Swart 2010: 20–24).

The Cape settlement now imported horses from the East and elsewhere. In 1689, it imported some 'Javanese' ponies (a South East Asian horse of Arab-Persian breed). It later introduced South American stock (in 1778); North American breeds (in 1792); English Thoroughbreds (in 1792) and Spanish Barbs (in 1807). Through breeding and acclimatisation, the Cape Horse/Pony evolved. It was exported to other parts of the world, while it also found its way into the hinterland of its own territory (Swart 2010: 32).

Wealth, Redistribution and Social Relations

Moshoeshoe's chiefdom grew and its population increased rapidly in the nineteenth century. From eighty thousand people in the 1840s, the population had reached about two-hundred thousand by the 1890s (Eldredge 1993: 94). Frequent outbreaks of war at the beginning of the century disrupted production and trade networks. As a result, the survival of the people depended heavily on their chiefs' ability to provide livestock and land for them. Moshoeshoe redistributed wealth in the forms of these two commodities to provide for his people. For Basotho, the land belonged to the people; it was held in trust by chiefs who had administrative rights over it, while the people had rights of usufruct (Duncan 2006). Commenting on land administration, ownership and use among the Basotho, Casalis (1861: 159) had this to say:

> The sale or transfer of land is unknown among these people. The country is understood to belong to the whole community, and no one has a right to dispose of the soil from which he derives his support. The sovereign chiefs assign to their vassals the parts they are to occupy; and these latter grant to every father of a family a portion of arable land proportionate to his wants. The land thus granted is insured to the cultivator as long as he does not change his locality. If he goes to settle elsewhere, he must restore the fields to the chief under whom he holds them, in order that the latter may dispose of them to some other person. The bounds of each field are marked with precision; and cases of dispute are referred to the arbitration of the neighbours; and, as a last resort, to the chief himself.

Furthermore, Moshoeshoe redistributed cattle to his subjects through cattle-loaning (*Mafisa*). He would loan a household about twenty to thirty heads of cattle. By 1839, Moshoeshoe had allocated around twenty thousand cattle in this way (Backhouse 1844: 375). The benefactor retained ownership rights and any offspring, and could inspect his livestock at any time. The recipient was responsible for grazing cattle in the mountains where there were good pastures. They consumed dairy products, and after the introduction of the plough, used oxen as draught power. Since cattle were spread over a wide geographical area, not all of them could be affected by drought or disease at once. Kimble (1978: 53) argues that 'by lending cattle to his followers, the chief could reduce the danger of over-concentration of stock, and gain access to a vast area of pasturage'. Casalis (1861: 155) observed that:

> Most of the flocks and herds captured in war become the property of the chief; and the subjects regarded it as a favour to become the depositaries and guardians of these new acquisitions. The milk belongs to them; they use the oxen as beasts of burden, and, from time to time, obtain permission to kill an animal which is already old; but they must always hold themselves in readiness to present the flocks to their real owner when he wishes to inspect them. When this favour is once granted, the chief cannot withdraw it without good grounds for so doing. Such is, in fact, the great social bond of these tribes; the sovereignty, instead of being supported by the community, are the chief supporters of it. In certain cases, such as a particularly difficult enterprise, or when vengeance is to be taken on an enemy who has caused all to suffer, the subjects have their share in the spoil. The chiefs, after having selected what they think proper, distribute the remainder. This largess is rare. Wealth, by change of hands, would endanger too much the stability of power. It is a fact, that the natives have been able to obtain cattle by performing services for the colonists (Afrikaners).

Moreover, through a patron-client system (*Bohlanka*), Moshoeshoe gave bridewealth (*Mahali/lobola*) to destitute young men and some warriors, allowing them to marry. The labour of any children of these marriages belonged to him, not to the biological parents. Moshoeshoe also enforced communal work parties (*Matsema*) for agricultural production and other community activities. The work parties produced food for the chiefs' senior wives, orphans, warriors and refugees (Mothibe 2002b: 18–20).

The chiefs controlled the deployment and activities of the work parties since they held administrative rights over the land. They allocated residential and agricultural lands to married men and controlled its seasonal use. Typically, wealthy men who were polygamists got more land. The work parties were indispensable to all phases of the production cycle (Ellenberger 1912: 266; Duncan 2006: 74–75). Eldredge (1993: 67) comments that: 'Chiefs allocated two or three fields to every man when he married. In return every man who had been allocated fields owed his allegiance to the chief'; and among other things 'he was obligated to work at the chief's work-parties …when certain designated fields of the chief were cultivated'.

To oversee his expanded chiefdom, Moshoeshoe created a fully functioning system of governance centred on the 'Court of Counsellors' (Lekhotla). This body had four major divisions. First, the ministers (*Matona*) were the 'eyes, ears and arms, of the chief' (Casalis 1861: 222). Second came the commanders of the armed forces (*Balaoli ba Mabotho*). Third were the diplomats (*Maqosa*); they were the chief's trusted messengers and negotiators. Last were the official doctors (*Lingaka*) of the chief. They acted as the chief's philosophers, wise men, intelligence gatherers, propagandists, community healers and initiation leaders. They performed protection rituals for the chief, community and warriors (Machobane 1990: 19–22).

As well as subjugating and co-opting weaker communities, Moshoeshoe formed alliances with stronger clans, such as the Bataung of Chief Moletsane and Baphuthi of Chief Moorosi, to expand his power over many communities, distant and close. These chiefs remained independent and collaborated during attacks. As I show later, Chief Moorosi affirmed his independence from Moshoeshoe until the end of the nineteenth century. He 'placed' his family members and close associates as chiefs over vast territories, while he co-opted and subordinated others by military means. Through a federated political system, he allowed his subordinates to run their affairs while he extracted tribute. It was only in the 1850s that he finally defeated and subjugated his long-standing arch-rivals, the Batlokoa (Thompson 1975; Sanders 1975; Seloma 1994).

In general, social and political relations remained complex, fragile, confrontational, collaborative and unequal in favour of Moshoeshoe, who emerged as an impressive and powerful leader in the post-Mfecane period, and his clan. He used different socio-economic and political strategies and institutions to centralise power in himself and his kinship network. In a context of regional conflicts and insecurity, most people had no option but to submit to the new political formation. In return, Moshoeshoe enjoyed support from the people because he allowed them a degree of freedom and autonomy.

During these early years, the chiefs competed for popular support, since people could 'vote with their feet' if a chief was oppressive. In one instance, Moshoeshoe's brother, Posholi, attempted to become a tyrant, but people laughed it off and Moshoeshoe did not encourage such behaviour. In relating the story, Casalis (1861: 219–20) said: 'In our days a petty Mosuto prince, named Poshuli [sic], took it into his head to set up for a second Chaka, and to exact homage due to a demigod'. To this end, he 'ordered, for instance, that when he appeared in public the vulgar herd, who assembled to gaze at him, should keep at a respectful distance'. He added 'that the stones which obstructed his path should carefully be taken out of the way … the pretensions of the petty king were merely laughed at'.

Various chiefs were also quite anxious because these were still the formative years, and many had not yet established their hegemony over the people. As Casalis (1861: 219–20) observed, much power rested in Posholi's 'elder brother (Moshoeshoe), whose head was better organised, and who would have treated the matter seriously if anyone had been punished for not conforming to this new etiquette'. In this sense, Moshoeshoe was a balancing force between the people and subordinate chiefs.

The chiefs could gang up against individuals who managed over time to accumulate wealth on their own. In such cases, more prosperous commoners were dispossessed. Ashton observed that the chiefs 'obstinately opposed economic development that might enrich and emancipate their subjects', and were fond of the predatory practice of '"eating up a person": namely, punishing a prosperous man for some misdemeanour by seizing all or the greater part of his stock' (1967: 220). Casalis confirms that the chiefs' practice of 'eating up a man' was upheld through the 'toleration of a certain offence until it is committed by an individual whose wealth can pay for all the delinquents' (1861: 219).

In general, various formations centralised power around the chieftainship and made the chiefs economically indispensable to their followers. In return, the people owed the chiefs their allegiance. In this context, the arrival of the missionaries in 1833 and their promotion of commerce offered some people a means of escape from the chiefs and their oppressive tendencies.

Missionaries, Commodity Production and New Trading Networks

Eugene Casalis and Thomas Arbousset were ordained in Paris in October 1832. Joined by Constant Gosselin, they set out for the Cape the next month, arriving in February. They were welcomed by Dr John Philip, a Superintendent of the London Missionary Society (LMS) based in the Cape, who was responsible for establishing relations between the interior and the Paris Evangelical Missionary Society (PEMS). The three young men aimed to work among the Batswana people, to the north-west of the region. From the Cape, they sailed for Port Elizabeth, where they were welcomed by Prosper Lemue and other LMS missionaries. They stayed there for some time learning about missionary life before they journeyed into the interior by ox wagon. On the way, they made a stop at Philippolis (Gill 1997: 7–10).

Named after Dr Philip, Philippolis was established by the LMS in 1823 as a mission station among the Griqua people, a semi-nomadic Afrikaans-speaking people of mixed-race origin. The three young missionaries had an encounter there that changed their destiny. With a group of other LMS missionaries, they met Adam Krotz, a Griqua hunter. Krotz had met Moshoeshoe, who wanted missionaries to work amongst his people. In relating his meeting with Moshoeshoe to the missionaries, Krotz said:

> While I was carrying on my hunting at a place eight days' journey from here, a chief sent two men to beg me to visit him. I took with me an interpreter, one of the natives of the country whom I had received on my farm. He conducted me to a mountain where this chief had fixed his residence, and who was, for this reason, called the Mountain Chief. His true name was Moshesh, son of Mokhatchane [sic].
>
> He told me that for several years past he had been a victim of incessant attacks … He had asked me there to know if I could give him any good advice, if I could show him any means of securing peace for the country. I thought at once of the missionaries; I spoke to him about Moffat and about our own men. I tried to make him understand the services which such men could render him.
>
> The idea of having near him permanently wise men, friends of peace, disposed to do all in their power to aid him in his distress, pleased him greatly. He wanted to have some at once. 'Do you know any?' said he to me, 'who would be disposed to come?' I replied that such men sometimes came our way. 'Oh, I beseech you, tell the first you meet to hasten here. I will give them the best possible welcome. I will do everything they advise me to do'. (Casalis 1889: 137–38)

Accompanied by Adam Krotz, the three missionaries arrived at Thaba-Bosiu to meet the Mountain Chief for the first time on 28 June 1833 (ibid.: 8). Thereafter, they established mission stations at Morija, Beersheba and Thaba-Bosiu in 1833, 1835 and 1837, respectively. The Evangelical missionaries opened the door for Roman Catholic missionaries, who arrived some twenty-nine years later; when they arrived in 1862, they were led by Bishop Allard and Father Joseph Gerard of the Oblates of Mary Immaculate. In 1876, Thomas Stenson and John Widdicombe led the Anglican Church into the mountain kingdom (Mothibe and Ntabeni 2002: 35–36). By 1843, the Christian community had increased to about four hundred, and by the end of the nineteenth century, about fourteen thousand in a population of some two hundred thousand had converted to Christianity (Eldredge 1993: 94).

The missionaries played a crucial role in the transformation of the local economy and society after the Mfecane wars. Significant changes took place in the first three decades. On arrival, they observed that: 'The trade which the natives [carried] on among themselves [was] not worthy to be enumerated as one of their means of existence. It [was] yet a very small matter' (Casalis 1861: 169). As a result, the missionaries promoted commerce by encouraging the people to produce for the market, and they tied the spread of the 'gospel' to commerce. Kimble points out that the missionaries promoted private property and individual rights to undermine some of the Basotho's customs, which had maintained the people's dependence on their chiefs. She argues that the missionaries aimed 'at the dissolution of the existing social relations [by] encouraging their followers to refuse to participate in the various forms of obligatory labour-service' (Kimble 1978: 106–8). She notes that the Evangelical missionaries 'explicitly tie[d] the propagation of the gospel to their encouragement of commodity production, particularly wheat, the consumption of European goods, and (wage) labour for the white colonists' (ibid.: 102).

The missionaries introduced the ox-drawn plough, domestic animals, some fruit trees, vegetables and grain varieties. The Basotho mostly cultivated sorghum, which was their staple food. It had four varieties. 'Oral tradition says BaSotho [sic] first acquired sorghum from their Nguni neighbours to the south', cites Eldredge (1993: 67). It could withstand dry seasons, unlike maize, which needed more care and rain. Maize was typically planted at the edges of the sorghum fields. Maize seems to have been acquired from the Nguni people on the eastern coast, who in turn had got it from the Portuguese; it also came from the Cape Colony (Casalis 1861: 214; Eldredge 1993: 68). The missionaries introduced more of its varieties, as well as wheat; however, it took time and effort for the Basotho to adopt wheat, which, like maize, needed lots of water. In 1835, the missionaries planted the first wheat crop, but it failed. Despite this, the missionaries continued to promote wheat, particularly for trade, and from the 1840s, more Basotho were beginning to grow this crop (ibid.).

The missionaries also introduced merino sheep and angora goats; the people valued these for the wool trade and used their fat to make soap and ointments. Pigs, cats, dogs and poultry were other new additions from the missionaries. The horse wagons that they introduced made transportation easier and could carry more loads across vast distances (Ashton 1967: 134–35). The mission stations became vibrant commercial centres for a new class of converted Christians (*Majakane*); these were a local elite group consisting of members of the royal family and some commoners. By the early 1830s, the Basotho had adopted more crop varieties and traded them with their African neighbours for livestock. Furthermore, they had insignificant numbers of cattle by the mid-1840s, but were exporting large herds to the Cape in the 1850s. In June 1838, Arbousset observed that: 'The Baralong, the Bahlaping, and the Griquas come daily to buy grain and to supply this nation with cattle; it was hitherto very poor in the latter' (Germond 1967: 439). Since the arrival of the missionaries, 'no fewer than 1,500 head [*sic*] of horned cattle, 40,000 sheep, 35,000 goats, 200 horses, 300 rifles and ammunition in corresponding amounts of powder and lead, have been imported' (ibid.).

During the 1830s, the Basotho still experienced severe crop failure due to locusts and drought. In September 1838, Samuel Rolland, founder of the PEMS missionary station at Beersheba, commented: 'Besides, it is well known that Africa is exposed to the terrible locust plague. Since my brother's arrival at Beersheba, he has not yet reaped more than a single harvest'. He added that: 'In 1835 and 1837, his wheat and vegetables were completely devoured'. Conditions were sometimes so dire that a 'year of drought is enough to reduce a herd by half. Last year Mr Pellissier lost 24 cows and 40 sheep' (Germond 1967: 439).

During the dry season, the Basotho could survive on stored grain, hunting, and trade to procure some necessities. In good years, they sold their surplus produce and stored significant amounts for the harsh and unpredictable seasons in the future. In June 1838, Arbousset remarked that: 'Stocks of millet have been stored in the capital to last seven or eight years; with other chiefs, four or five' (Germond 1967: 439). Supporting this, François Daumas (founder of the Mekoatleng mission station) advanced in May 1838 that 'the inhabitants have had the good fortune to reap a fairly abundant harvest; they are now busy cutting their wheat and sorting it in grass baskets'. He emphasised that the baskets were 'so skilfully woven that, although exposed to the elements the whole year round, they remain impervious to the rain' (Daumas cited in ibid.).

Basotho trading activities increased with the arrival of Afrikaner groups from the Cape in the interior of the region. Following their mass exodus from the Cape in the late 1830s and 1840s, Afrikaners settled in the territory claimed by Moshoeshoe and beyond, later naming it the Orange Free State. This was not their first time in the interior: they had seasonally grazed their animals deep into the fertile plains of the region (Feinstein 2005; Swart 2010). Moshoeshoe granted the Afrikaners temporary grazing rights when they first arrived in the 1830s and 1840s. This was common practice and the Basotho saw them 'as mere passers-by' (Mothibe and Ntabeni 2002: 43).

At first, Moshoeshoe saw the Afrikaners as a buffer between his people and his enemies on the western side, particularly the Ndebele people of Mzilikazi and the mounted Griqua commando units. As a result, relations between the Basotho and the Afrikaners were relatively friendly during these early years and were characterised by exchanges of commodities, while many Basotho worked for the Afrikaners (Mothibe and Ntabeni 2002).

Equipped with new agricultural technologies, the Basotho became major players in the new regional economy. They were now connected to the world through the Orange Free State and the seaports, particularly the Cape Colony and the Eastern Cape. From the mid-1830s, most of their trade was conducted with the Afrikaners, who depended on the British to supply guns, ammunition and other European goods. The Afrikaners supplied the coastal areas with grain, wool, cattle and skins in return, which they procured from the Basotho (Casalis 1861: 170; Keegan 1986: 198). The Evangelical missionaries' Annual Conference Report of May 1842 noted: 'Civilization continues to make great progress … the inhabitants have strongly applied themselves to the cultivation of European corn, they sell it to the farmers who barter it for cattle, clothes, soap, salt etc' (Germond 1967: 441).

Basotho bought soap, salt, arms and ammunition, cattle and horses from the Afrikaners, and some manufactured goods such as clothes, utensils, iron hoes and saddles from the British (Casalis 1861: 170; Keegan 1986: 198). In May 1854, Thomas Arbousset wrote that the British 'admired Moshoeshoe's character, appreciated his power and influence, and admit that his nation supplies them with the best shepherds', and that his country had 'grain and cattle in abundance. Therefore, they seek his friendship and he theirs, in consequence of which this country is, without comparison, more peaceful and minds calmer than heretofore' (Germond 1967: 229). In 1858, a British trader based at the Morija mission station sold to the Basotho about 1,000 overcoats, 220 pairs of trousers, 220 jackets, 1,200 shirts, 200 hats, 350 saddles, 500 bridles, 500 stirrups, 200 shoes, 7,300 knives, 8 ploughs, 1,500 hoes, 150 iron saucepans, and 6 wagons (F. Maeder, cited in Mothibe and Ntabeni 2002: 41).

The Basotho were so significant within this trading network that the 'Eastern Cape was heavily dependent on Basotho grain supplies, and during the frontier wars of the late 1840s and 1850s, "enormous quantities" of wheat were imported from Basutoland', and by the 1850s, they 'had also become large-scale exporters of livestock and horses' (Keegan 1986: 198). Missionary accounts celebrated 'Basutoland … [as] the granary of the Free State and of part of the (Cape) Colony' (Lemue, cited in Germond, 1967: 459). Casalis observed that: 'The corn which is brought from the country of the Basutos to the markets of the colony is remarkable for its extreme purity … It is with white men that the natives transact the most profitable business'. He added: 'In this respect, the Basutos are particularly favoured by the fertility of their country' (Casalis 1861: 169–70).

In May 1854, Arbousset observed that the mission station of Morija was a favourite hub for Basotho producers and their customers, particularly from the Orange Free State (Germond 1967: 451).

The Basotho's economic opportunities expanded further with the discovery and exploitation of diamonds in Kimberly. In 1867, alluvial diamond deposits were found at the confluence of the Vaal and Harts Rivers in the dry plains west of Bloemfontein. By 1870, some five thousand people flocked in from the region and the world to make their fortunes. Within two years, their numbers had increased to fifty thousand. Individual diggers acquired small plots and employed labour-intensive methods and technologies to unearth diamonds. By this time, four major mining areas took shape, but they were subdivided into smaller claims, with Kimberly being the largest (Shillington 1989: 317).

The Basotho took advantage of the commercial opportunities that came with the discovery and exploitation of minerals, and consequent industrialisation, by supplying labour and grain to the populations of the new mining towns (Germond 1967: 322–24; Murray 1980, 1981). Basotho began to take up employment in the mines, and at first, because of their relative affluence and labour competition between South African firms, many could set their own terms of employment. They moved easily from one employer to the next and could choose how to be paid; many preferred guns. In southern African historiography, these early labour movements are termed 'discretionary labour migration' due to the degree of independence and voluntarism that people exercised (Thabane 2002: 108; Eldredge 1993: 147).

Basutoland became the 'granary' of some of the South African mining towns (Murray 1981). While compiling the *Chronicles of Basutoland* in Paris, Paul Germond came upon this missionary account: '[In 1873, the] populations which have profited most from the discovery of the diamond beds are those which, comparatively far from them, have assiduously applied themselves to agricultural pursuits' (Germond 1967: 323). And elsewhere: 'The Basuto of our stations witness the daily influx in their midst of crowds of people, who do nothing else but buy the wheat and other food crops, with the object of selling them again to the mines' (ibid.).

In 1874, Paul Germond[2] noted, 'although far removed from the main current of events, the Basuto have nonetheless reaped their share of the general prosperity'. He added: 'The price of cereals has doubled, their flocks are multiplying and wool commands a good price; as money is easily earned, people are better clothed, the traditional hut is being superseded by more comfortable dwellings …' (Germond 1967: 324). Despite wars and frequent drought spells, by the 1860s and 1870s the Basotho were prosperous to a point that worried the missionaries. They were afraid that what they called 'the love of gain' would turn the Basotho away from their religious obligations and beliefs. In May 1873, Dr Eugene Casalis, son of the first Casalis, noted that:

> A danger which now threatens our churches and to which we must draw your attention, is the love of gain. Basutoland is traversed in every direction by the wagons of traders who, in exchange for their money and their commercial ware, convey to the diamond fields and the Free State, Europeans and native corn, also the maize which the Basuto grow on a vast scale. The high prices which their cereals command, and the ease with which their produce is sold, tend to favour among them the love of money; material interests are in danger of turning many souls away from spiritual values. (Germond 1967: 322)

Summary

The missionaries' promotion of commerce upon their arrival was transformative, and their activities revitalised trade in the post-Mfecane period. A new group of entrepreneurs that produced for the markets emerged in and around the mission stations, selling commodities to local and distant markets. With commerce, early forms of labour migration became an alternative to an economy dominated by the chiefs, who controlled the allocation of land and livestock to sustain power.

This emergent class used money and markets to emancipate itself from the oppressive chiefs. After European contact, the Basotho adopted new economic and military technologies (particularly horses, guns and agricultural innovations) that gave them various advantages over many African communities in the region. Despite wars and droughts, they rose to be significant actors in the new regional economy and politics. Hierarchical, regional economic formations of this time were founded on interdependence, trade and shifting alliances based on mutual interests and democratic aspirations.

Therefore, money, markets and people connected the domestic economy to the region at large. The influences of various actors ensured that the Basotho interests were met; but if such was not the case, militant conflicts were inevitable. Basotho could stand their own ground. In its own way, Moshoeshoe's nation-building vision was hierarchical and inclusive. He formed alliances with different groups within and outside his territory, and he allowed his people to participate in trade and labour markets to build their own wealth. Towards the late nineteenth century, economic individualism was simultaneously developing and fast replacing religious and collectivist principles that had made the earlier successes possible. Social cohesion weakened, allowing for external forces to dismantle economic independence. These were fertile grounds for colonialism, as is chronicled in the next chapter.

NOTES

1. Mzilikazi was the king of the Matebeleland, which forms part of modern-day Zimbabwe. He left the Zulu Kingdom with his followers during the Mefcane wars. Sekonyela ruled the Batlokoa people in the Highveld, and was Moshoeshoe's arch-rival. Dingane was the king of the Zulu people (1828–40). Hintsa was king of the Xhosa people in the modern-day Eastern Cape Province.
2. Sent by the Paris Evangelical Missionary Society, Paul Germond arrived in Lesotho in 1860. His grandson Robert Germond compiled the *Chronicles of Basutoland* using missionary and colonial records.

REFERENCES

Ambrose, D. n.d. 'Oxfam Guide to Thaba-Bosiu', Unpublished Report. National University of Lesotho Archives.

Ashton, H. 1967. *The Basuto: A Social Study of Traditional and Modern Lesotho.* London: Oxford University Press.

Backhouse, J. 1844. *A Narrative of a Visit to the Mauritius and South Africa.* London: Hamilton Adams.

Casalis, E. 1861. *The Basutos: Or, Twenty Years in South Africa.* London: James Nisbet & Co.

Duncan, P. 2006. *Sotho Laws and Customs.* Morija: Morija Museum and Archives.

Eldredge, E.A. 1993. *A South Africa Kingdom: The Pursuit of Security in Nineteenth Century Lesotho.* Cambridge: Cambridge University Press.

Ellenberger, D.F. [1912] 1992. *History of the Basuto: Ancient and Modern.* Morija: Morija Archives and Museum.

Feinstein, C.H. 2005. *An Economic History of South Africa: Conquest, Discrimination, and Development.* Cambridge: Cambridge University Press.

Germond, R.C. 1967. *Chronicles of Basutoland: A Running Commentary on the Events of the Years 1830–1902 by the French Protestant Missionaries in Southern Africa.* Morija: Morija Sesuto Book Depot.

Gill, S. 1993. *A Short History of Lesotho: From the Late Stone Age until the 1993 Election.* Roma: National University of Lesotho, Institute of Southern African Studies.

Hamilton, C. (ed.). 1995. *The Mfecane Aftermath: Reconstructive Debates in Southern African History.* Pietermaritzburg: University of Natal Press.

Hamilton, C., B.K. Mbenga and R. Ross. 2012. *The Cambridge History of South Africa, Volume I: From Early Times to 1885.* Cambridge: Cambridge University Press.

Keegan, T. 1986. 'Trade, Accumulation and Impoverishment: Mercantile Capital and the Economic Transformation of Lesotho and the Conquered Territory, 1870–1920', *Journal of Southern African Studies* 12(2): 196–216.

Kimble, J. 1978. 'Towards an Understanding of the Political Economy of Lesotho: The Origins of Commodity Production and Migrant Labour, 1830–1885', MA dissertation. Roma: National University of Lesotho.

Machobane, L.B.B.J. 1990. *Government and Change in Lesotho, 1800–1966: A Study of Political Institutions*. London: Macmillan Press.

Mothibe, T. 2002a. 'Early Communities of the Southern Highveld, 1500–1800', in N.W. Pule and M. Thabane (eds), *Essays on Aspects of the Political Economy of Lesotho, 1500–2000*. Roma: Department of History, National University of Lesotho, pp. 1–14.

______. 2002b. 'State and Society, 1824–1833', in N.W. Pule and M. Thabane (eds), *Essays on Aspects of the Political Economy of Lesotho, 1500–2000*. Roma: Department of History, National University of Lesotho, pp. 15–34.

Mothibe, T., and M. Ntabeni. 2002. 'The Role of the Missionaries, Boers and British in Social and Territorial Changes, 1833–1868', in N.W. Pule and M. Thabane (eds), *Essays on Aspects of the Political Economy of Lesotho, 1500–2000*. Roma: Department of History, National University of Lesotho, pp. 35–57.

Murray, C. 1980. 'From Granary to Labour Reserve: An Economic History of Lesotho', *South African Labour Bulletin* 6(4): 3–20.

______. 1981. *Families Divided: The Impact of Migrant Labour in Lesotho*. Cambridge: Cambridge University Press.

Omer-Cooper, J.D. 1987. *History of Southern Africa*. California: University of California.

Parsons, N. 1993. *A New History of Southern Africa*. Midrand: Macmillan.

Sanders, P. 1975. *Moshoeshoe, Chief of the Sotho*. Sandton: Heinemann.

Seloma, T. 1994. 'Subordination and Co-option: The Mokoteli Dynasty and its Relationship with other Chieftaincies in the Lesotho since the Nineteenth Century', MA dissertation. Roma: National University of Lesotho.

Shillington, K. 1989. *History of Africa*. London: Macmillan Education.

Swart, S. 2010. *Riding High: Horse, Humans and History in South Africa*. Johannesburg: Wits University Press.

Thabane, M. 2002. 'Aspects of Colonial Economy and Society, 1868–1966', in N.W. Pule and M. Thabane (eds), *Essays on Aspects of the Political Economy of Lesotho, 1500–2000*. Roma: Department of History, National University of Lesotho, pp. 103–130.

Thompson, L. 1975. *Survival in Two Worlds: Moshoeshoe, 1786–1870*. Oxford: Clarendon Press.

Walton, J. 1959. *Lesotho: Basutoland Notes and Records – Volume 1*. Morija: Morija Printing Works.

CHAPTER 2

The Loss of Economic Independence, 1870s–1890s

Introduction

Basotho precolonial economic autonomy and general prosperity deteriorated in the second half of the nineteenth century. The European encounter had other consequences beyond catalysing trade. For the Basotho, their downfall began with the loss of their land to the Afrikaners. Moshoeshoe had allowed the latter to occupy his lands for customary and strategic reasons (see Chapter 1), but soon relations changed between these groups, leading to conflicts and wars over land in the mid-century. This in turn facilitated subsequent British intervention and colonisation. The rise of the Basotho nation was also characterised by turbulence; at first, they held their ground, but they became British subjects in 1868.

In their migrations into the region, both Basotho and Afrikaners found the San, as we saw previously. Unlike the San, the two groups held more rigid claims to the land, based on who arrived first. The Basotho emphasised collective ownership of land and its resources, and the Afrikaners set store by private titles. Based on racist ideologies, the Afrikaners failed to recognise the Basotho as their equals. They had left the Cape because they were against the British anti-slavery reforms. The result was perpetual conflicts between the Afrikaners and the Basotho, and regional conditions that had allowed both to coexist and trade fragmented. By the mid-century, war and conflict were fast replacing commerce. In turn, this constricted movement of goods and people.

The British annexed Basotho territory at the time when minerals were discovered in South Africa. With shrinking opportunities in commerce, more Basotho leaned towards labour migration, and due to their general economic independence, they could dictate terms of employment. They moved from one employer to the next in search of better pay and conditions. Those who had built enough resources to participate in the markets supplied grain and livestock to the emergent mining towns. They had their fair share of prosperity; however, the economy was fast shifting away from its collectivist nature. Increasing economic individualism even worried the missionaries who had supported Basotho emancipation from the chiefs.

In a context of land shortage and growing economic individualism, the Basotho became divided. Their efforts to resist colonialism fell short as a result. They could no longer defend their long-term economic interests, even with guns, and an emergent materialistic impulse made them more susceptible to manipulation by rulers. The chiefs aligned with colonial authorities that worked to dismantle Basotho economic independence and create cheap labour from the Basotho.

In the last three decades of the nineteenth century, the British became more aggressive in order to meet increased labour demand in the mines (Arrighi 1973; Bundy 1979; Murray 1980, 1981). Environmental catastrophes and Afrikaner protectionist measures played a significant role in confirming the Basotho's status as cheap labour. This chapter brings together a myriad of factors which contributed to the destruction of a regional economy based on co-dependence; I emphasise the collapse of Basotho economic independence, as well as the origins of a rigid colonial bureaucracy which was used to extract labour and structure commerce. In an adapted form, and with added violence, postcolonial governments inherited this system. Its legacy in the underdevelopment of Africa lives on.

British Annexation of Basotho Territory

Conflicts over land between the Basotho and the Afrikaners arose when the latter made moves to occupy land permanently. Contrary to the Basotho's land-tenure system, customs and wishes, they turned land into private property and transferred it among themselves. As a result, in October 1844, Moshoeshoe sent a warning letter telling them to halt private transfers of land. He declared: 'All purchases and sales already made or under the process of being made, of farms, springs, houses, kraals and other immovable structures are contrary to our laws and customs and therefore illegal and null and void' (Theal 1883: 81). The Afrikaners ignored his threats.

Both groups herded animals and competition for pastures led to fierce altercations. The Afrikaners acquired more land, and even encircled missionary stations in the western parts of the territory, hindering missionary activities. The missionaries believed that their evangelism and the gospel were an integral part of industrial civilisation – something that the Afrikaners lacked in their opinion. The Afrikaners had opposed the British anti-slavery crusade and legislation and left the Cape as a result (Mothibe and Ntabeni 2002: 44–45).

Casalis advised Moshoeshoe to seek British intervention and protection. He wrote to his friend in the Cape, Dr Philip, who was close to George Napier, the Governor of the Cape Colony (1838–44). Napier responded positively to their plea. From the 1840s, the British assumed the role of mediators and arbiters between Moshoeshoe and the Afrikaners. This took the form of diplomatic negotiations, proclamations, boundary demarcations, awarding land leases to the Afrikaners and constant negotiations with the Basotho. As a result, the latter lost a substantial part of their territories (Mothibe and Ntabeni 2002: 47).

The British approach to mediation prioritised peace and stability. Accordingly, they persuaded Moshoeshoe to make a series of land concessions to the Afrikaners as a condition of their alliance. This made the Afrikaners' permanent appropriation of the land legitimate. In 1843, the Cape Governor passed the Napier Treaty on a 'take-it-or-leave-it' basis. Moshoeshoe was forced to promise to be a faithful ally, to maintain the peace and to co-operate with the British in 'civilising' his people. This included capturing and returning any criminals or fugitives from the Cape (Thompson 1975: 117–25).

The Napier Treaty undermined Moshoeshoe's ability to rule independently. For his loyalty, he received an annual commission of either £75 sterling or arms and ammunition, as he chose. The treaty stirred up internal conflicts. After the British colonised Natal, more Afrikaners flooded into the Mohokare Valley with demands for land. The new governor of the Cape, Peregrine Maitland (1843–47), repealed the Napier Treaty in June 1845 while trying to find a plausible solution. He proclaimed Basotho lands occupied by the Afrikaners 'alienable' and those retained by Basotho as 'inalienable'. The same year, Major Henry Douglas Warden was appointed as the first British Resident in Bloemfontein; among other things, he was tasked with resolving Basotho–Afrikaner land conflicts. In his six years in office, he did nothing to alter the Maitland Treaty (Mothibe and Ntabeni 2002: 47–49).

In February 1848, the British under Harry Smith established the Orange River Sovereignty (ORS) by annexing disputed territory between the Vaal (Lekoa) and Caledon (Mohokare) rivers with the aim of imposing direct control. The Afrikaners resented this development, and in July they launched a rebellion against the British, which failed. Conflicts persisted, especially after Major Warden drew a new boundary line in 1849. This boundary separated various chiefdoms, thereby pitting the chiefs against each other. Moshoeshoe's authority was undermined further. The Basotho responded by raiding the Afrikaners' livestock, refusing to move and deliberately relocating to the 'wrong' side of the Warden line. As a result, in June 1851, the Basotho and the British went to war for the first time; the Basotho defeated the British, thereby ending Warden's career. In 1852, British forces under George Cathcart suffered a further defeat at the hands of the Basotho, this time in the Battle of Berea (Mothibe and Ntabeni: 52–53).

Thereafter, the British changed their strategy. In 1852, they granted the Afrikaners self-rule under the Sand River Convention and imposed on Africans a more stringent arms embargo than before. In 1854, they gave the Afrikaners independence under the Bloemfontein Convention, making the Orange Free State official. From the outset, relations between the Basotho and the Free State were characterised by hostility and conflict, and in 1858, they went to war against each other. The Basotho were victorious, but they also felt the impact of the arms embargo. From the early to mid-1860s, the economy was sluggish. Droughts and locusts destroyed crops, and the Afrikaners suffered the most, since unlike the Basotho, who could draw on their more fertile lands, they had few stores of grain. Feeling the pressure, they attacked the Basotho in 1865 and 1867. Natural disasters and the arms embargo led to defeat for the Basotho; they were forced to sign the Mpharane and Thaba-Bosiu Treaties in 1866, which awarded almost 80 per cent of their fertile lands to the Afrikaners (Mothibe and Ntabeni: 54).

In 1868, the British finally annexed what was left of Basotho territory, and it officially became Basutoland. Soon afterwards, in March 1870, Moshoeshoe died at Thaba-Bosiu, aged 84. The British had two major strategic and economic interests driving the annexation. First, persistent conflicts between the Basotho and the Afrikaners disrupted trade; as a result, the British officials in the region saw the annexation of Basotho territory as a solution. Philip Wodehouse, the British High Commissioner in the Cape, wrote to convince his superiors in London that it was economically prudent to appropriate the Basotho's territory. In his letter of May 1868, he wrote that annexation of the territory was 'the best guarantee we can take against future disturbance' because 'our commerce will no longer be ruined by their quarrels' (as cited in Theal 1872: 300).

Second, the British saw the Basotho as a militarily powerful chiefdom in the Mohokare Valley, capable of checking the Afrikaners' expansion. They were particularly keen to stop the Afrikaners from reaching the seaports, which would give them more autonomy (Theal 1883: 170). After escaping from British rule in the Cape, the Afrikaners had set their sights on Port Natal, a move not favoured by their arch-rivals. The British conquered Natal in 1843 and declared it their colony. They then turned Moshoeshoe's territory into a buffer zone and a means to control the region. 'Britain harboured fears that if the Boer commandos conquered Lesotho, the Free State would have had access to a seaport at Port St. Johns in the Eastern Cape', observes Thabane (2002a: 91).

Access to seaports of their own would reduce the Afrikaners' dependence on the British-controlled seaports. 'Specifically, the Free State would be able to import arms and ammunition without having to secure permission from British officials in the Cape'. If that became the case, Thabane adds, 'it would make redundant the one weapon that the British had used over the years to maintain their supremacy in the region; namely, a balance of power in which they controlled the weights' (2002a: 91).

Colonial Rule in the Creation of a Mines Labour Reserve

By the 1870s and up until the mid-1880s, mining became difficult for individual white diamond diggers, who were typically assisted by three or four black labourers. Excavations had deepened so that mining now required more sophisticated technologies and a larger labour force. As a result, competition intensified to the point of cut-throat rivalry. Three young fortune-seekers eventually consolidated their operations in a monopoly company, De Beers Consolidated Mines. The young entrepreneurs – Cecil Rhodes, Barney Barnato and Alfred Beit – arrived in 1869, 1873 and 1875 respectively. Between 1890 and 1896, Rhodes was the Prime Minister of the Cape Colony (Thompson 1990: 115–17).

In 1886, rich gold deposits were discovered between the Limpopo and Orange Rivers in what became the Witwatersrand. By this time, the minerals revolution was in full swing, and individual diggers were quickly being replaced by large joint-stock companies. In 1889, mining industrialists formed the Witwatersrand Chamber of Mines to consolidate their grip over regional and global markets for minerals. By the turn of the century, European capital investment was about £60 million. The mines contributed 28 per cent of global gold output and employed about one hundred thousand black people (Thompson 1990: 119–20).

The British took advantage of their global economic superiority to consolidate their power within the region. They completed their conquest of the Afrikaner republics (the Free State and Transvaal) and the African communities within the region – the Zulus, Xhosas, Sothos, Swazis, Tswana and others. The new mining industry generated a high demand for labour, and colonial authorities became more aggressive in extracting labour from these Indigenous communities. They pulled them into the capitalist nexus, subjugating resistance through violence and war. Coercion became a routine feature of the system.

When it became a British Protectorate in 1868, Basutoland was placed under the High Commissioner, Philip Wodehouse, while James Henry Bowker became the country's first Governor's Agent. When Bowker arrived in 1868, he stationed his police post at Mokema, between Thaba-Bosiu and the Morija mission station. He moved to Maseru in March 1869, and next to the Caledon (Mohokare) River in the central western lowlands. Maseru – a place of creamy sandstone – subsequently became the central colonial administrative town through which district magistrates were controlled. Since then, it has been the country's capital (Ambrose 1993: 35–36).

Wodehouse's approach to imposing colonial laws was that they should be introduced gradually in order not to provoke Basotho hostility. In 1871, the country was handed over to the Cape Colony, and the Cape government imposed colonial laws more aggressively (Thabane 2002a). Their purpose was to create a labour-reserve economy. A Hut Tax became one of the primary means of forcing Basotho into supplying labour for the mines in order to earn wages.

The British method was indirect rule, with some administrative powers devolved to chiefs and head men. The imposition of this system meant that chieftainship was strengthened and centralised in the Paramount Chief;[1] accordingly, Basotho groups were subjected to Moshoeshoe's lineage. The British were eager to promote the idea that various groups living in a colonised territory were to be put 'under one Family', as Henry Barkey, High Commissioner and Governor of the Cape Colony, expressed it (Theal 1872: 290).

British rule was contested, not only by some of Moshoeshoe's allies (such as Moorosi) but also by his children. Moshoeshoe had identified as his successor his oldest son, Letsie. But his two other senior sons, Molapo and Masupha, refused to recognise their older brother. While growing up, both, especially Masupha, had shown keen interest in their father's political affairs, demonstrating their managerial ability. Letsie turned out the opposite way. Molapo and Masupha held that their father had risen to his position by merit and not by birthright. In this context of intense succession politics, the British installed Letsie as the Paramount Chief in 1870 (Thabane 2002b: 124). Masupha retained the central Thaba-Bosiu stronghold, forcing Letsie to relocate to Matsieng, a village a few kilometres away from the Morija mission station; Molapo meanwhile moved to Leribe, in the north of the country.

In 1871, the British annexed the territory of Chief Moorosi in the southern highlands. Although dominant, the Mokoteli lineage had not completely consolidated its power as the Basotho's uncontested monarchy before the country became a British Protectorate. Some groups considered themselves allies, but not subjects, of Moshoeshoe. The Baphuthi of Chief Moorosi were one such group. Both the colonial government and Letsie considered Moorosi to be an unruly rebel; they claimed that 'he was not always a very obedient vassal' (Germond 1967: 332). To demonstrate his autonomy, Chief Moorosi persistently described himself as 'totally emancipated from Moshoeshoe' (Ajulu 1979: 34). His 'rebellious' proclivities posed a problem for the colonial government, which sought to centralise authority under one chief for ease of control.

When the colonial government attempted to expand reliance on cash and to introduce colonial laws, Moorosi had been the first to challenge these arrangements openly (Ajulu 1979: 34). The British introduction of a Hut Tax in 1870 was decisive. The colonial regime insisted that the tax should be paid in money, not in kind as had been the case before. The shift to money-based tax payments was so rapid that the Governor's Agent commented that 'in 1870, the first year that the Hut Tax was collected, several thousand sheep and as many 'muids'[2] of grain were received in lieu of money'; and that 'last year only a few hundred sheep and as many muids of sheep were collected'. The Agent concluded that 'this year I think the Hut Tax will be paid almost entirely in money' (Theal 1872: 500).

Chief Moorosi held that the use of money would destroy the social fabric of Basotho society. Speaking to the commercialisation of traditional beer, he warned: 'You know that if people begin selling beer, then travellers will suffer hunger if they don't have money to buy … I know it will be extended to bread' (as cited in Ajulu 1979: 34). This was only the beginning of Moorosi's resistance to colonial rule and to the imposition of rule by the Mokoteli lineage.

Basotho Resistance to Colonial Rule: The Moorosi Rebellion and the Gun War

In 1877, the colonial government divided the Cornet Spruit – a territory in the southernmost parts of the country – into two. The newly created district of Quthing belonged to Chief Moorosi, who vehemently rejected this colonial imposition. As far as he was concerned, Moshoeshoe, not he, had asked for British protection. As a result, relations between him and the newly appointed Resident Magistrate, Hamilton Hope, were hostile. Following an incident in which a rifle misfired, accidentally killing a person at a public gathering (*Pitso*), Hope banned guns from public gatherings. Moorosi disregarded this, commenting: 'When a bull goes out to pasture, he does not leave his horns in the kraal' (Eldredge 2007: 45).

Hope's frustration with Moorosi was exacerbated when the Magistrate's office called a public gathering to read colonial laws to the people after his arrival in July 1877. As Charles Maitin, a colonial official, was reading the laws, Moorosi became increasingly irritated, to the point that he stood up and asked his people: 'Are you my people, or are you the Government's people? If you are Government people you are fools. Do you obey this man (pointing at Hope) or do you obey me? They all with one voice cried out, we obey Morosi [sic]' (Eldredge 2007: 43). Hope stormed angrily out of the gathering, leaving behind Maitin and accompanying policemen and constables.

Following rumours that Moorosi was planning to expel Hope, the Cape Colonial Affairs Office sent a letter to him, in which the Secretary for Native Affairs, William Ayliff, threatened war against Moorosi. For a time, the latter exercised restraint, but this was short-lived. His oldest son, Doda, led violent altercations that culminated in Moorosi's eventual death and the subjugation of the Baphuthi. Hope imposed a Hut Tax on four Baphuthi widows; Doda rejected this and assembled a small army, promising to fight if the government attempted to make any arrests. In April 1878, about eighty of Doda's men attacked the constables sent to confiscate two head of cattle as tax payment and fled with the animals. The government issued a summons against Doda and others. Doda openly refused: 'I have nothing to do with Makhooa (white people); I only know Moorosi' (Eldredge 2007: 50–51).

The following month, a Disarmament Bill was tabled before the Cape Parliament. In August 1878, the Bill received Royal Assent as the 'Peace Preservation Act' (Act 3 of 1878). The Act was an attempt to 'remove an obvious temptation to resist lawful authority and even rebellion' (Ajulu 1979: 36). In October 1879, the new Cape Prime Minister, Gordon Sprigg, held a public meeting in Maseru to inform the Basotho that they were to be disarmed. Sprigg infuriated the Basotho further when he also announced that the tax would be increased from 10 shillings to £1. He added that the government intended to alienate the Baphuthi's territory from the rest of Basutoland and allocate it for European settlement (ibid.: 36-42). Not surprisingly, Moorosi, Masupha and some other dissident chiefs condemned this disarmament (Thabane 2002b: 104–105).

In October 1878, Colonel Griffith became the Governor's Agent, and Hope was replaced by John Austen as Resident Magistrate of Quthing.

Austen pulled no punches; with the colonial government's backing, he targeted Moorosi, intending to punish the whole group. He jailed Doda, his two brothers and their men at Aliwal North in the Free State, and confiscated relatives' livestock as punishment for aiding the fugitives. During the festivities and drunkenness of the following New Year's Eve, Moorosi's men broke Doda and others out of prison (Eldredge 2007: 67–69).

The Cape authorised military intervention to punish Moorosi and his people, and with support from Paramount Chief Letsie I, they successfully defeated the Baphuthi. Following the prison break, the latter had prepared for war; they drove their animals into the mountains and took their women and children to safety. They then attacked the colonial government's offices, looted a trading store and confiscated the property and stock of colonial loyalists. Austen fled. The Governor's Agent, Griffith, wrote to various districts and chiefs seeking their military intervention. He put a bounty of two head of cattle on Moorosi, and approved the raiding of livestock during the battle (Eldredge 2007: 67–69).

In November 1879, the Cape Colony mounted a surprise attack at night on Moorosi and his men, who were hidden in a cave at the top of his mountain fortress. As a result, they captured them with little resistance, while others, including Doda, escaped. Dying of gun wounds, Moorosi had a 'curiously disdainful smiling expression' (Eldredge 2007: 69). No doubt he despised bondage up to his death. The Cape soldiers decapitated Moorosi; his head was taken to Kingwilliamstown, but the colonial office ordered that it be returned to be buried with his body.

Although they were against war and more bloodshed, the missionaries were opposed to the disarmament of the Basotho. They proposed instead a tax on guns as a way of reducing their popularity. With assistance from Adolphe Mabille, a Swiss Evangelical missionary and Eugene Casalis' son-in-law, Letsie sent a petition to the Queen of England in January 1880. The Cape would not budge. Reverend Mabille owned the only printing press in Basutoland at the time, and despite Sprigg's threats, he refused to translate and print the government's Peace Preservation Act for wider circulation (Storey 2008: 287–318).

Despite the Basotho's strong resistance and their military potential, the Cape proceeded with its strategy and passed the Peace Preservation Act in April 1880. Their victory over Moorosi had only increased their arrogance. The Act forced the Basotho to surrender all their guns to local magistrates in return for monetary compensation. About half of the adult male population owned guns. The majority refused to comply, and by July 1881, were attacking and confiscating the property of those who had returned their guns.

The Basotho termed these loyalists the 'Matikita' – a term derived from the 'tickets' that they received upon surrendering their guns. In fact, the government was forced to return their guns so that they could protect themselves against the aggression of their fellows. Fearing for the loyalists and for European lives, Letsie requested arms and ammunition from the Cape to protect them. He also asked that the loyalists be allowed to rent farms in the Free State, but his efforts fell on deaf ears. Sprigg held that only military punishment could restore law, order and obedience in Basutoland (Storey 2008: 287–318).

In September 1880, a contingent of colonial Cape Mounted Rifles arrived in Basutoland, and the first battle of the Gun War was fought. Between then and February 1881, Cape regiments fought against Molapo, Masopha and Lerotholi in different places. The Cape forces suffered some two thousand casualties during this period. The Cape colonial government had borrowed more than £1,300,000 from Standard Bank, without security, to fight the war, and when the war ended in April 1881, it had cost the British about £3 million (Thabane 2002b: 111; Storey 2008: 315–16).[3]

In the course of the war, Sprigg continued to demand that the Basotho adhere to the Peace Preservation Act, but the chiefs refused. The Orange Free State prohibited the selling of arms and ammunition to Basotho, but this only established an underground trade whereby some Afrikaners continued to sell them. Despite significant property damage and loss of life, the Basotho took full advantage of their mountainous topography and fought back aggressively against the Cape forces. The House of Assembly in the Cape was forced to pass a motion of no confidence against Sprigg. Sprigg's government collapsed and he was replaced by Thomas Scanlen.

The British suffered a massive defeat, but they were able to attain their long-term goals in partnership with some dominant chiefs. They played a significant role in consolidating Moshoeshoe's lineage of Mokoteli as the uncontested monarchy of the country, determining the politics of succession and swaying outcomes to suit their interests. They supported the installation of 'obedient' figures, to rule the Basotho within the colonial system of 'indirect rule'.

Consolidation of Colonial Rule

Following the Gun War, the Basotho had the option of choosing to be independent. However, with an eye to Afrikaner aggression across their border, they decided to remain under British protection. From 1884, the Governor's Agent was replaced by a Resident Commissioner, who reported to the British High Commissioner in the Cape. District Magistrates were replaced by District Commissioners. In January 1884, Colonel Marshal Clarke was sent from Britain to assume the position of Resident Commissioner. He brought with him Sir Godfrey Lagden as Secretary, Accountant, and Assistant Commissioner. J.C. Macgregor became the Police Officer and later Assistant Commissioner (Eldredge 2007: 118).

The Basotho's choice allowed the British to consolidate their rule. They strengthened their system of indirect rule, using the Paramount Chief as a figurehead. This allowed them to manipulate succession in the Mokoteli family, although conflicts still existed between Moshoeshoe's sons. In 1891, Letsie died, and with British backing, Lerotholi succeeded him (Eldredge 2007: 34).

Masopho continued to be a strong chief and was popular with the Basotho. He vehemently opposed colonial meddling in domestic politics. On his arrival in 1884, Lagden observed that Basotho were 'willing to be governed … But the success of Masupha in defying authority was a serious bar to unity. He was able to centralize disaffection and detach a strong body of ardent rebels who kept alive opposition to any form of government and hatred of the loyals' (Eldredge 2007: 119). In 1897, the British endorsed Lerotholi's use of force against Masupha following a series of land conflicts. His defeat ended contestations over the royalty and resistance to colonial law (ibid).

In 1903, the colonial government pushed for the establishment of a National Council to consolidate its rule and system of chiefship. The Council functioned as a 'parliament' and sat once a year, and was intended 'to deal with tribal affairs in consultation with the government' (Stevens 1967: 35). The Council had a maximum of one hundred members, with five nominated by the Resident Commissioner and the rest by the Paramount Chief, and the Resident Commissioner was its permanent President.

Increased land disputes around 1900 were fuelled by population increase, land shortage, soil degradation and a number of environmental and economic catastrophes. These buttressed the colonial government's aim to turn Basutoland into a cheap labour reserve for South African mines. In the 1870s and 1880s, following the fixing of borders and imposition of colonial rule, Basotho working in South Africa, and some of those residing in conquered territories, had flocked into Basutoland from the Orange Free State, Transkei and Natal along with their property and livestock.[4]

By the 1890s, the previously uninhabited mountain areas were populated by permanent residents cultivating crops along the slopes; these areas were previously used as seasonal grazing lands (*Metebo*). The country experienced severe drought from 1894 to 1898. In the 1890s, crops were attacked by several plagues of locusts, and in 1891, the rinderpest epizootic culled four fifths of Basotho cattle. The inevitable result was famine at fluctuating levels of intensity (Murray 1980).

The cattle epizootic persuaded South Africa[5] to deploy protectionist measures, including halting importation of livestock from Basotho and other African communities. In 1893, the Free State imposed tariffs on grain from Basutoland to protect Afrikaner farmers who had turned to crop production. When railway lines linking coastal areas with the interior were completed in the 1890s, South Africa began importing cheaper grain from Australia (Murray 1980). Temporary relief for the Basotho came from the outbreak of the second Anglo–Boer War (1899–1902). Basotho supplied grain and horses to both sides during the war, with about twenty thousand horses coming from Basutoland. In 1901, horses constituted some three quarters of the country's export market value (Swart 2010: 94–96).

After the war, when the British and the Afrikaners formed the Union of South Africa in 1910, the Basotho, Batswana and Swazis were to be incorporated. However, they resisted, instead remaining British High Commission territories. In June 1910, Britain and South Africa engaged in negotiations that resulted in the formation of the Southern African Customs Union (SACU) in Potchefstroom, a city in South Africa. Their aim was to maximise revenue collection at a regional level and share it proportionally (Ettinger 1974: 59). SACU collections are derived 'from purchases of all foreign (mostly South African) goods and services, collected into a common pool' (Wellings 1985: 194).

The 1910 arrangement consolidated previous customs union agreements. In 1889, the British Cape Colony and the Boer Republic of the Orange Free State had established what is today the world's oldest customs union agreement, and in 1891, they were joined by British Bechuanaland and Basutoland, and subsequently by the Bechuanaland Protectorate and Natal in 1893 and 1899, respectively (Wellings 1985; Lundahl and Peterson 1991; Usa 2009; Rossouw 2016).

Labour Recruitment to the Mines

In 1892, about twenty thousand labour passes were issued to Basotho to work in the mines. By 1904, out of a population of some three hundred and fifty thousand, more than eighty-six thousand Basotho men worked in the mines. These numbers increased after a railway line connecting Maseru to South Africa was completed in 1906 (Stevens 1967: 39). Effectively, from the beginning of the twentieth century, most Basotho depended on wages from South Africa; from then on, the country could no longer be described as an agricultural society. Instead, it was a labour reserve (Murray 1980).

Arriving with an Australian contingent, Ernest Stephens (1876–1951) landed in South Africa during the Anglo–Boer War. In 1915, he moved to Basutoland to exploit its business opportunities, and there found George Hobson, one of the leading figures in Maseru. Stephens established a trading store – Mafafa Store – and owned the country's only hotel. The homes of these two men were a hub for social events, especially for the whites-only Civil Service Club and the Basutoland Chamber of Commerce (see Chapter 3).

Labour recruitment made Stephens' fortune. He arrived when Basutoland was well-established as a labour reserve, coming with two other Australians, Willats and Maitland Brown, to exploit opportunities in the mines-labour business. In 1932, Stephens leased his hotel to focus on trading and labour recruitment. He 'once boasted that he had recruited over 100,000 labourers during his recruiting career' (Ambrose 1993: 143). The name of his store, 'Mafafa', was also the nickname given to him by Basotho. It meant that 'he gave bags of money to chiefs who provided him with large numbers of their men for the mines' (ibid.: 135).

The Mafafa Store stood near the region's biggest labour-recruiting company, the Native Recruitment Corporation (NRC). The agency opened an office in Maseru in 1931 and subsequently established more branches across the country. Led by the biggest agency, Eksteens, private labour-recruiting agencies in South Africa had formed this corporation in 1912 (ibid.: 135).[6]

Smaller labour-recruitment agents were spread across Basutoland, but Stephens and the NRC monopolised the lucrative opportunities for mines recruitment, while these agencies recruited for a variety of European interests – farms, factories, railways and others. Basotho women mostly left their country to work on farms or as domestic servants, or to earn a living through informal enterprises, selling food and beer (Ashton 1967: 162–65).

Summary

The regional economic configuration that had sustained both the Basotho and the new arrivals ultimately ended, and the collapse was disastrous for the Basotho. The discovery of minerals was a turning point and heralded the emergence of a new epoch. Effectively, the post-Mfecane society, with its successes and challenges, ended. The Basotho endured the consequences of land conquest and colonial violence. In pursuit of riches, the British abandoned the moral mission of the global anti-slavery movements; from then on, colonialism shaped economic relations in exploitative ways.

A striking feature emerges within Basotho society during this period. Economic individualism seeps into the social fabric, making the Basotho susceptible to strategic external manipulation. Money and markets continue to perform the role of connecting Lesotho to the regional economy; but the two become drivers of dire inequality. Compared to the earlier period, we see money and markets working against the people. In particular, the British deploy a punitive taxation system as one of the means to dismantle Basotho economic independence. As a result, the new economic configuration becomes rigidly dual and restrictive. The little that individual mine workers earn is used to support families and subsistence agricultural production, and to meet various cultural obligations pertinent to social reproduction back home.

Among the major drivers of the new colonial economy were bureaucracy and colonial laws, which played a critical role in structuring the economy and politics of the new labour reserve enclave. The administration used the chiefs to maintain law and order while the latter also became the conduit for the extraction of labour in return for various rewards. As a result, the chiefs now predominantly served colonial interests. In the rest of this book, we see that this formation was inherited in the postcolonial period.

NOTES

1. The term 'Paramount Chief' was used within the British colonial system to denote the highest-level ruler within a colonised society in the nineteenth and twentieth centuries.
2. 'Muid' is a French word; its English equivalent might be 'hogshead', a large cask used to measure liquids or solids.
3. The same year, 1879, the British went to war against the Zulus. For the Anglo–Zulu War, Standard Bank had lent the Cape Government no less than £400,000 a month.
4. Today, areas such as Bloemfontein (Magaung), Senegal, QwaQwa, Thaba-Nchu and many others are the homes of many Basotho groups who opted to stay in the Orange Free State.
5. In 1910, the British Colonies and Boer Republics merged to form the Union of South Africa after the Anglo–Boer War.
6. In 1977, NRC merged with the Witswatersrand Native Labour Association (WNLA). Africans popularised the acronym as 'Wenela'. Together, they became The Employment Bureau of Africa (TEBA). Established in 1902, WLNA mainly recruited from Mozambique.

REFERENCES

Ajulu, R. 1979. 'The Gun War in Basutoland, 1880–1881: Some Aspects of the Destruction of the Natural Economy and the Origins of Articulation', BA dissertation. Roma: National University of Lesotho.

Ambrose, D. 1993. *Illustrated History of Maseru.* Morija: Morija Museum and Archives.

Arrighi, G. 1973. 'Labour Supplies in Historical Perspective: A Study of the Proletarianization of the African Peasantry in Rhodesia', in G. Arrighi and J. Saul (eds), *Essays on the Political Economy of Africa.* New York: Monthly Review Press, pp. 180–234.

Ashton, H. 1967. *The Basuto: A Social Study of Traditional and Modern Lesotho.* London: Oxford University Press.

Bundy, C. 1979. *The Rise and Fall of the South African Peasantry.* Michigan: Heinemann.

Eldredge, E. 2007. *Power in Colonial Africa: Conflict and Discourse in Lesotho, 1870–1960.* Wisconsin: The University of Wisconsin Press.

Ettinger, S.J. 1974. *The Economics of Customs Union between Botswana, Lesotho, Swaziland and South Africa.* Michigan: University of Michigan.

Lundahl, M., and L. Peterson. 1991. *The Dependent Economy: Lesotho and the Southern African Customs Union.* Oxford: Westview Press.

Mothibe, T., and M. Ntabeni. 2002. 'The Role of the Missionaries, Boers and British in Social and Territorial Changes, 1833–1868', in N.W. Pule and M. Thabane (eds), *Essays on Aspects of the Political Economy of Lesotho.* Roma: Department of History, National University of Lesotho, pp. 35–57.

Murray, C. 1980. 'From Granary to Labour Reserve: An Economic History of Lesotho', *South African Labour Bulletin* 6(4): 3–20.

Murray, C. 1981. *Families Divided: The Impact of Migrant Labour in Lesotho.* Cambridge: Cambridge University Press.

Rossouw, M. 2016. *The Harmonisation of the Rule on the Recognition and Enforcement of the Foreign Judgements in the Southern African Customs Union.* Pretoria: Pretoria University Law Press.

Stevens, R.P. 1967. *Lesotho, Botswana, & Swaziland: The Former High Commission Territories in Southern Africa.* London: Pall Mall Press.

Storey, W.K. 2008. *Guns, Race, and Power in Colonial South Africa.* Cambridge: Cambridge University Press.

Swart, S. 2010. *Riding High: Horse, Humans and History in South Africa.* Johannesburg: Wits University Press.

Thabane, M. 2002a. 'The Nature of Social Relations in the Nineteenth Century', in N.W. Pule and M. Thabane (eds), *Essays on Aspects of the Political Economy of Lesotho.* Roma: Department of History, National University of Lesotho, pp. 59–77.

———. 2002b. 'Aspects of Colonial Economy and Society, 1868–1966', in N.W. Pule and M. Thabane (eds), *Essays on Aspects of the Political Economy of Lesotho.* Roma: Department of History, National University of Lesotho, pp. 103–30.

Theal, G.M. [1872] 2002. *Basutoland Records 1871–1872: Volume VI.* Roma: National Institute of Southern African Studies, University of Lesotho.

———. 1883. *Basutoland Records: Volume I.* Cape Town: Struik.

Thompson, L. 1975. *Survival in Two Worlds: Moshoeshoe, 1786–1870*. Oxford: Clarendon Press.

Thompson, L. 1990. *A History of South Africa*. New Haven: Yale University Press.

Usa, I. 2009. *South African Customs Union (SACU) Investment and Business Guide*. California: International Business Publications.

Wellings, P. 1985. 'The "Relative Autonomy" of the Basotho State: Internal and External Determinants of Lesotho's Political Economy', *Political Geography Quarterly* 4(3): 191–218.

Part II

British Trading Monopoly and the Liberation Struggle

CHAPTER 3

Colonial Commerce, 1870s–1930s

Introduction

This chapter chronicles the development of 'colonial commerce'. The last three decades of the nineteenth century, and the first three of the twentieth century, were foundational to this project. With the routinisation of labour migration, commerce – retailing and wholesaling – emerged as the pillar of the domestic economy. Mostly dependent on wages, this retail industry met the Basotho's everyday consumerist ends.

The installation of colonial rule from the beginning of the 1870s changed the organisation of local trade. In contrast to a less hierarchical and less strictly controlled form of trading (see Chapter 1), the government introduced bureaucratic reforms and laws to formalise trade. It aimed to abolish informal ways of trading and to confine trade to specific and regulated enterprises, as part of a newer form of trade that emerged with industrial capitalism in Europe.

I demonstrate that these institutional changes coincided with the arrival of a more entrepreneurially aggressive British cohort who came to dominate trade while excluding Basotho and Indian traders, the latter newly arrived from Natal and the Free State. The available literature on Lesotho's commerce – in the form of the two biographies of the Frasers Company by Walton (1958) and Danziger (1979) – covers the activities of European traders. These volumes chronicle the challenges and successes of European traders in Basutoland. However, the two authors neglected the political aspects of European traders' organisation and alliance with the colonial administration. Manipulating colonial laws and bureaucratic processes, the European traders and colonial officials together established an exclusive, unjust, exploitative, restrictive and oppressive form of commerce – 'colonial commerce'. Instrumental in this was their association, the Basutoland Chamber of Commerce. The British then monopolised retail and wholesale trade and recruitment to the mines, as we have seen.

Development of Enterprises

When the Afrikaners left the Cape Colony in the 1840s, they were among the first European groups to establish enterprises in the interior of the southern Africa region. Three traders opened trading stations at Platberg, where they traded for grain grown in Newlands (Nieuwland), between Platberg and Berea. Platberg was an area about 5 or 6 kilometres from the modern Maseru border post, on the way to Ladybrand in the Orange Free State. Formerly known as Makulukameng, it was settled by Wesleyan Methodist missionaries in 1833, and became a populous and busy trading centre in the Mohokare Valley (Ellenberger 1912; Ambrose 1993, 2009: 1–5).

In 1839, James Backhouse, a missionary from the Evangelical Society of Friends on his way to Thaba-Nchu, enjoyed the hospitality of a young couple, William Christian and Susan Bauer, who traded with the Afrikaners at the Sand and Modder rivers where there were good pastures. Some traders also established themselves around Thaba-Bosiu in the 1830s; James Forrey was said to be the first trader to open a store there. Later, traders such as Falconer[1] and an unnamed German trader also established their stores near the mountain (Walton 1958: 14). In line with Basotho land tenure, Moshoeshoe and his chiefs would grant traders 'permission' and land to establish their businesses.

From the 1870s, the number of European trading stations increased in the country. In 1871, there were twenty European-owned stores, and had reached thirty the following year. In 1875, the colonial government reported that 'the trade of this territory continues to increase. New trading stations are being erected every year' (Walton 1958: 16). By 1878, there were fifty of these trading stations – all owned by Europeans (Danziger 1979: 20).

Soon, Indian traders also started making inroads into Lesotho. Following the abolition of slavery in the British colonies in 1833, sugar-producing countries experienced an acute labour shortage. In the 1840s, Indians began to migrate to places like Mauritius, as indentured labour bound to a limited contract in exchange for free passage. Large numbers migrated to Natal (South Africa) from the 1860s, mainly from Madras, Calcutta and Hyderabad. They signed five-year contracts; when these ended, they had the option to return home or to stay in Natal for other economic opportunities (Hart and Padayachee 2000). Between 1895 and 1914, a second wave of Indians migrated to South Africa as traders; employed by members of the commercial class in Bombay and Gujarat, these were the 'Passenger Indians' (Du Bois 2012).

In South Africa, Indian traders spread throughout the country, and by the late 1880s, they had arrived in the Orange Free State. Indian businesses thrived to the point of being a threat to white traders. By 1885, Indian traders were selling at very low prices, so their white counterparts could not compete. Feeling the pressure, European traders complained to the government, and the authorities in Natal and the Free State took steps to undermine Indian traders. The Free State government passed an ordinance to prevent Indians from buying or renting any fixed property. With no compelling reasoning, President Jan Brand ordered the Indian traders to sell their merchandise within a period of two years, and to close their stores in 1887 (Rantheba 1985: 4–5).

Due to these exclusionary measures taken against the Indians in South Africa, many Indian traders tried their chances in Lesotho and elsewhere in the region. By this time, some were already hawkers, peddling their wares between Lesotho and South Africa. By 1911, some 180 Indian traders lived in Lesotho.[2]

Formalisation of Trade and Consolidation of Colonial Trading Law

The Cape colonial government introduced new trading laws and regulations, including the Mercantile Law of 1871. This new law made it obligatory to have a licence issued by the colonial government to conduct trade (Thompson 1961: 855). The laws were amended by Act 8 of 1879 before the outbreak of the Gun War. The first and crucial clause of the law read: 'No person shall be allowed to trade … in Basutoland unless he shall first have obtained a licence for that purpose from the Governor's Agent or from a magistrate in Basutoland' (ibid).

The law defined trading as any form of economic exchange or bartering. For wholesale and retail business operations, a license was granted to operate in a fixed trading station at a place approved by the colonial authorities. The new colonial laws gave the government the power to grant, refuse, renew and transfer licenses, and to punish any transgressor by imprisonment, a fine or both. At the time, a license cost £10 and was paid annually (Theal 1872: 124–27).

When the country was handed back to Britain, the colonial administration passed the Trading Regulations Act of 1884 to amend and enforce the previously promulgated laws. The regulations enforced several changes: procedurally, applications for a trader's licence and a business site were made to the Resident Commissioner in Maseru; Assistant Commissioners in charge of districts received applications in their districts and passed them to the Resident Commissioner. After his decision, applicants received responses to their applications through Assistant Commissioners.[3]

Second, the amended laws made it legal for any police officer, or any person authorised by the Resident Commissioner or Assistant Commissioner, to demand licences from traders at any time. Third, they allowed traders with licences to move freely across the new colonial borders. Basotho exporting grain out of the country for sale, however, were required to obtain a pass for two shillings and six pence. Failure to produce a pass meant liability to a fine not exceeding £1, or imprisonment up to one month. Lastly, licences could not be transferred between consenting parties without consulting the Resident Commissioner or Assistant Commissioners. In such cases, a fee of two shillings and six pence was to be paid.[4]

In 1918, the colonial government passed Proclamation No. 30 to consolidate all laws related to trade. This effected several changes. The Proclamation established a specific trading licence, the General Dealers' Licence, which permitted its holder to venture into any form of trading, including opening stores, operating a mill, selling wool and mohair, and hawking.[5] The Proclamation, however, prohibited trade in guns, ammunition and liquor. As a result, these were smuggled across the border instead (Ashton 1967: 167).

Furthermore, the Proclamation created a dual business-site application process. The Resident Commissioner allocated business sites in the town centres (known as Camps, or *Kampong*) and the Paramount Chief in the areas outside the towns. The towns were the most lucrative urban areas and colonial administration centres, and were dominated by Europeans.

Moreover, the Proclamation established a Licensing Board vested with powers to advise and assist the Resident Commissioner in granting, refusing, renewing and transferring licences, as well as addressing any grievances. This devolved the powers and duties of the Resident Commissioner. The Board consisted of three civil servants; the High Commissioner in the Cape appointed two board members and the chair annually, through a notice in the government gazette. The third member was the Assistant Commissioner of any district in which an application was made.[6]

The Licencing Board also hosted periodic meetings at which those supporting or opposing an application argued their case. After considering arguments for and against the granting of a licence, the Licensing Board made its decision.[7] European traders – particularly through their association, the Basutoland Chamber of Commerce – used this platform to advance their interests and to exclude aspiring Basotho and Indian traders. Thanks to their cordial relations with the government, European traders dominated the Licensing Board sittings. This chapter and the two following it deal with this process in greater detail.

The Rise of Frasers

In March 1877, Donald Fraser bought his first store, at Liphiring in the south-western part of the country (Danziger 1979: 18). His father, William Fraser of Ipswich (in England), had been a prominent wool merchant since 1837 and owned a prosperous business called William Fraser & Company. In the 1860s, Donald Fraser arrived in East London as a representative of his father's company. However, demand for the expensive and sophisticated Victorian type of clothing they dealt in was low in South Africa. In the economic boom after the discovery of diamonds at Kimberley, Donald Fraser moved into the interior to establish trading stores as an alternative. Douglas Fraser, his brother, joined him shortly afterwards. The Fraser brothers then acquired more stores in Basutoland, and by 1880, they were described as the 'leading traders in the territory' (Walton 1958: 21).

The Frasers took advantage of the Gun War and the diamond price recession that followed it (1882–83). European traders had been among the first to recognise that the war was coming; many of them abandoned their stores, taking their merchandise and property out of Lesotho into the Orange Free State. Fearing that the traders' exodus would create panic in the country, the colonial government threatened to remove the trading licences of those who left and to not allow them to return after the war. This discouraged the exodus to a degree. Those who stayed still sent their families away for safety, while the men remained to defend their stores (Walton 1958: 21).

The Gun War brought trade to a standstill. Stores were damaged, and in some instances ruined. Basotho participation in the war was not unanimous; some complied with the colonial authorities' demands and agreed to return their guns, as we have seen. In 1882, a delegation – consisting of Charles D. Griffith (a former Governor's Agent in Basutoland), J.A. Burger (the chairman of the delegation), A. Auret and Cecil John Rhodes (who was also a member of the Cape parliament at that time) – was mandated to inquire into the losses of 'loyal' Basotho, missionaries and European traders. The Cape government compensated their Basotho supporters, but European traders received nothing. The delegation argued that the colonial government was not responsible for their losses; instead, it recommended that they take insurance to be protected against future catastrophes.[8] Several European traders could not re-establish their stations. Many were eager to sell, and the Fraser brothers took full advantage of this situation (Walton 1958: 29).

At the same time, diamond prices slumped in the world market. In the resulting economic depression, trade levels dropped, since Lesotho's exports fetched low prices in South Africa. Consequently, more trading stations closed; their numbers fell from eighty-two to seventy-three in 1882 and 1883. In the district of Mafeteng alone, seven stores closed. The Fraser brothers bought stores when they closed, and formed a company called D. & D.H. Frasers Limited, which continued to acquire more stores around the country (Walton 1958: 29–33). To consolidate their power, the two brothers invited other European traders of British descent to join their firm in 1920, which by then was established as Frasers Company, and thereafter simply as Frasers.[9]

Consolidation and Domination: The Role of the Basutoland Chamber of Commerce

In September 1890, European traders held a meeting to discuss how they might counter the economic hardship they had faced since the Griffith–Auret–Rhodes Commission had excluded them. The result was the establishment of the Basutoland Traders' Association, which was to protect their interests in times of economic recession and war, and to represent them collectively in local commercial matters. Membership of the association was open to European traders only. In September 1893, they changed the name of the organisation to the Basutoland Chamber of Commerce (Ashdown 1961: 1; Ambrose 1993: 101). The Chamber became a powerful colonial organisation that could influence the issue of trading licences by the government, and it was instrumental in consolidating European traders' dominance over local commerce, functioning as a quasi-branch of the colonial government while being informally controlled by Frasers. It dominated Licensing Board meetings.

Trade only picked up again in the country during the Anglo–Boer War (1899–1902), owing to the return of Basotho and Afrikaner refugees from the Orange Free State. Several aspiring Basotho traders applied for trading licenses in order to take advantage of this opportunity, but few obtained them because of strong opposition from the Chamber. The latter argued that there were more than enough trading stations in the country (Walton 1958: 34–35). In 1902, George Hobson, the chairman of the Chamber, wrote:

> [T]he improvement in trade was mainly due to the advent of a large number of Dutch refugees and Natives from the Orange River Colony, but on the return of peace, all these people will return to their homes, and local trade will resume its usual hum-drum character. (As cited in Walton 1958: 50)

That same year, the Chamber wrote to Paramount Chief Lerotholi to convince him not to allow new licences to be issued. Although he was undecided at first, he responded in a letter to the Resident Commissioner agreeing to the traders' request. Part of this response read as follows: 'Whereas we have already agreed, I say that I am not in favour of new shops being established. Those that are already in the country are enough' (cited in ibid.: 36). Because of the objections voiced by the Chamber of Commerce, the colonial government turned down many trader applications.

The commercial boom caused by the Anglo–Boer War came to an end, and the regional economy was stagnant in the interwar period. This was because of plagues of locusts, droughts and the global economic depression (Pim 1935: 60).[10] The collapse of international demand for South Africa's mineral and agricultural exports was reflected in Basotho migrants' wages and purchasing power. Business was 'hard hit by the recent fall in prices since the main exports – wool, mohair and cattle – could not fetch profitable prices in the markets. Between 1932 and 1933, there was a severe famine across the country' (Pim 1935: 61). As a result, the role of the Chamber was pivotal in protecting European interests.

In October 1923, the Chamber successfully lobbied the government to give it a list of traders' licence applications and transfers across the country two weeks before they were posted on the public notice boards.[11] The reasons given for and against a trading licence application contributed significantly to the decision on whether it was granted, according to colonial trade laws and regulations. This was of course at the Board's discretion, and if arguments against an application were backed by many established traders or their organisations, the application would fail.[12] The Chamber's request read: 'The Basutoland Chamber of Commerce through its Governing Committee are anxious to have a list of all applications for General Trader's Licences or Transfers which may be appearing on the Notice Boards', in the districts of 'Qacha's Nek, Leribe, Quthing, Mohale's Hoek, Mafeteng and Berea'.[13]

Acting in violation of the law, the Resident Commissioner sent a circular to all Assistant Commissioners and Officers-in-Charge in those districts, instructing them to give extra copies of all traders' licence applications and transfers to the Chamber of Commerce. Thus, armed with the list of applications in advance, the Chamber tightened its grip on commerce, as with this information it could oppose any application and counter its arguments with ease.[14]

In January 1924, the Chamber further convinced the colonial government to allow its committee to 'have the prerogative of addressing Assistant Commissioners up to the time of sittings of the Licencing Board'.[15] With these expanded privileges, the Chamber could protect its interests by acting as an informal special adviser to the colonial government.[16]

Later, when more Basotho had broken into local commerce, they requested similar privileges. This time, however, the colonial government denied them these prerogatives. In July 1927, Thomas Mofolo, one of the early Basotho traders, a renowned literary scholar and a member of the Basuto Progressive Association (see Chapter 5), wrote to the government requesting that Basotho traders be given a list of all traders' licence applications as well. In the letter, Mofolo complained that the lists of applications and transfers were frequently posted very late on the notice boards, meaning that Basotho traders could not prepare their arguments well in advance. The government refused and directed the Basotho to follow procedure, saying: 'His Honour the Resident Commissioner regrets that your request cannot be granted', and pointing out that: 'A notice of all such applications is posted on the Notice Board in the District concerned for public information in terms of the Proclamation'.[17]

The Chamber worked assiduously to block any new licence applications from Indians, Basotho and any white outsiders. Before long, Indians in Lesotho posed the same threat to Europeans as they had done in South Africa. In fact, many had strong economic and kinship networks, tied to rich merchants in Natal and India. In May 1916, the Resident Commissioner wrote to the High Commissioner in South Africa complaining that the Indian traders had 'substantial means, representing a large amount of capital. Many are commercially connected with, and in some cases are branches of large wholesale Indian firms in Natal'.[18]

The colonial government and the Chamber took steps to frustrate the Indians. Their typical strategy was to reject their traders' licence applications. In September 1918, the Indian traders submitted a petition to the High Commissioner in South Africa. They complained that two Indian traders had attempted to apply for trading licences in a town centre, but that their applications had been refused – only for licences to be granted subsequently to European traders. The authorities ignored their complaint.[19]

The colonial government employed yet another strategy to undermine competition from the Indians: it confined them to operating in selected areas, namely the Botha-Bothe and Leribe districts in the north-western parts of the country. The government also issued them licences to operate in the remote rural highlands outside the urban lowlands and town centres dominated by Europeans (Rantheba 1985: 14).[20]

The Indians soon understood the monopolistic tendencies of European traders. Not long after migrating to Lesotho, they formed an organisation: the Basutoland Mahommedan Community, a body through which they hoped to voice their collective grievances.[21] This was not a business association as such, but one which represented them in various political, social and economic matters.[22] Their efforts, however, did not amount to much against the power exercised by the Europeans and the colonial government.[23]

Thomas Mofolo applied for a trading licence in May 1923 in the town centre of Teyateyaneng (TY); in refusing his application, the Licensing Board, chaired by J.P. Murray and with R.B. Smith and J.H. Sims as its members, wrote:

> The Board having duly considered all the arguments in favour of and against this application considers that the actual centre of Teyateyaneng is sufficiently well catered for by the four existing stores … the Board feels that by [*sic*] granting any further Licences in Teyateyaneng will only lead to disaster. The application is therefore refused.[24]

Frasers, Cyril Collier, Dare & Glynn, Jacot-Guillarmod, Morus Bros Ltd, Mr C. Tully and Yeats & Co all had stores in the centre and in the adjacent villages of 'Mamathe and Mapoteng (Walton 1958: 39).

Additionally, the Resident Commissioner rejected an application from one M.E.F. Wessels from Winburg (South Africa) in April 1930. Wessels, an Afrikaner, wished to establish a business in Lesotho; however, he was an outsider and not a member of the Chamber of Commerce. Acting on advice, the Resident Commissioner claimed that 'in view of the present state of trade depression there is very little likelihood of any new licences being granted in the near future' because 'the needs of the country are sufficiently met by the existing stores'.[25]

Against the united front of the colonial government and the Chamber, some applicants were only successful following a protracted struggle. An aspiring Mosotho trader, George Kou, first applied for a licence in 1930. After several attempts and fierce opposition from European traders, he was finally granted a licence in 1935. In opposing his first application, A.J. Yeaman, a member of the Chamber, wrote to the Licensing Board, arguing that: 'I am advised by my Chamber that a native by the [name] of George Kou has applied for a licence at Nkesi's Chief Api's ward. I wish strongly [to] oppose the granting of this Licence'.[26] Another member of the Chamber, A. Scott, added:

> I have the honour to lodge the following objection in reference to a General Trader's Licence applied for by George Kou at Abel's Village Sethleketseng [sic] in Maseru district. I beg to submit that in the area named there are more than sufficient Trading Stations to cater for the needs of the local and mountain populations even if no depression in trade existed.[27]

In 1935, the Maseru district had thirty-two stores, all owned by Europeans. George Kou's store was an addition to this (Pim 1935: 60).[28] Countrywide, European traders had 194 licences, Indians sixteen and Basotho three (ibid.). The Pim Commission observed that: 'European traders have played a large part in the development of the country … [They, however,] have naturally concentrated in the main on their own special interests'. It added that: 'Very few new licences have been granted during the last twenty years … more than one-third of the 194 stores appear to be controlled directly or indirectly by two large firms and their influence extends even more widely so that competition has largely ceased to operate' (ibid.).

Summary

By the turn of the century, Basutoland had two dominant economies: commerce (comprising Europeans and Indians) and labour migration (comprising Basotho). European traders took advantage of the newly imposed colonial laws and regulations to undermine competition from the Indians and Basotho. Through their Chamber, they systematically crafted an impenetrable economy: 'colonial commerce'. They laid the foundation for a rigidly defined 'national economy' dependent on consumer goods coming from the outside the country.

Commerce has emancipatory potential; we saw this in Chapter 1. As a result, it went against colonial interests to create cheap labour out of the Basotho. The colonial government and European traders assiduously worked together to exclude Basotho from commerce, and Indians could operate in only selected areas, a measure enforced to undermine their competition. By the mid-1930s, only a few Basotho had broken into local commerce, but outside lucrative town centres; they were instead issued licences to operate in remote and sparsely populated mountainous regions. Colonial commerce depended on a rigid colonial bureaucracy to thrive, and the British used colonial law and bureaucracy to exclude other groups. Based on unequal terms, commerce connected Lesotho to the global imperial economy, as part of the exploitation of the continent as a whole.

NOTES

1. Attempts to find Falconer's first name have been unsuccessful. Here, as in the rest of the study, where I could not find first or last names, I have used only the available name.
2. *Lesotho National Archives* (hereafter LNA), *Trade, S3/14/1/4*, Indian Traders' Petition to the Resident Commissioner in Lesotho, 23 September 1918.
3. *LNA, Basutoland High Commissioners' Proclamations and Notices: From 12 March 1868 to June 30*, 1909, 80.
4. *Basutoland High Commissioners' Proclamations and Notices*, 80–110. This source, together with other *Proclamations and Notices* referenced in this study, are from the National University of Lesotho Archives.
5. *Basutoland Proclamations and Notices, 1918.*
6. *Basutoland Proclamations and Notices, 1918*; Proclamation No. 4 of 1919, *Basutoland Proclamations and Notices, 1919.*
7. Trade Regulations promulgated under Notice No.1 of 1929, *Basutoland Proclamations and Notices, 1929.*These regulations were added on top of the principal law relating to trade, which was Proclamation No. 28 of 1928.
8. *LNA, Report and Proceedings of the Government Commission on Basutoland Losses*, 3–9.
9. *LNA, Trade, S3/26/1/2*, Frasers Company Registration Documents, 24 March 1920.
10. *LNA, Trade, S3/26/1/8–11*, Letters of the Basutoland Chamber of Commerce, and those of its individual members, to the Resident Commissioner, Maseru, 1927–32.
11. *LNA, Trade, S3/26/1/4*, Basutoland Chamber of Commerce to Government Secretary, Maseru, 30 October 1923.
12. *LNA, Trade, S3/26/1/5*, Basutoland Chamber of Commerce to Government Secretary, Maseru, 8 December 1923.
13. *LNA, Trade, S3/26/1/4*, Basutoland Chamber of Commerce to Government Secretary, Maseru, 30 October 1923. Lesotho now has ten districts. Including Botha-Bothe, those listed in the Chamber's request were the main districts at the time; Mokhotlong and Thaba-Tseka districts were later additions.
14. *LNA, Trade, S3/26/1/5*, Basutoland Chamber of Commerce to Government Secretary, Maseru, 8 December 1923.
15. *LNA, Trade, S3/26/1/6*, Basutoland Chamber of Commerce to Government Secretary, Maseru, 23 January 1924.
16. *LNA, Trade, S3/26/1/1*, Proceedings of the Licensing Board Meeting, Maseru, 27 May 1919; *LNA, Indian Immigration, S3/14/1/3*, Petition of the Basutoland Indian Association to the Assistant Commissioner, Botha-Bothe, 23 September 1918;

LNA, Trade, S3/26/1/11, Resident Commissioner in Maseru to M.E.F. Wessels of Winburg, South Africa, 8 April 1930.
17. *Trade, LNA, S3/26/1/10*, Government Secretary in Maseru to Thomas Mofolo of Teyateyaneng, 11 July 1927.
18. *LNA, Indian Immigration, S3/14/1/2*, Resident Commissioner in Maseru to the High Commissioner in South Africa, 4 May 1916.
19. *LNA, Indian Immigration, S3/14/1/2*, Indian Traders' Petition to the High Commissioner in South Africa, 20 May 1913.
20. *LNA, Indian Immigration, S3/14/1/3*, Indian Traders' Petition to the Resident Commissioner in Maseru, 26 May 1918.
21. Due to a lack of records, little is known about the history and other activities of this association, or even when it was formed.
22. *LNA, Indian Immigration, S3/14/1/1*, List of Committee Members of Basutoland Indian Association, 20 November 1916.
23. *LNA, Indian Immigration, S3/14/1/4*, Indian Traders' Petition to the Resident Commissioner in Maseru, 26 May 1918.
24. *LNA, Trade, S3/26/1/5*, Decision of the Licensing Board Meeting, Teyateyaneng, 3 May 1923.
25. *LNA, Trade, S3/26/1/11*, Resident Commissioner in Maseru to Mr M.E.F. Wessels of Winburg, 8 April 1930.
26. *LNA, Trade, S3/26/1/9*, Mr A.J. Yeaman of Morija to the Assistant Commissioner, Maseru, 23 May 1930.
27. *LNA, Trade, S3/26/1/9*, Mr Scott of Mohale's Hoek to the Assistant Commissioner, Maseru, 23 February 1931.
28. *LNA, Basutoland Progressive Association, S3/22/1/1*, George Kou to Basutoland Progressive Association, Morija, 20 September 1935.

REFERENCES

Ambrose, D. 1993. *Illustrated History of Maseru*. Morija: Morija Museum and Archives.

———. 2009. *Wesleyan Methodist Church: Lesotho Annotated Bibliography Section 45*. Ladybrand: House 9 Publications.

Ashdown, J.R. 1961. 'Basutoland Chamber of Commerce', Address at the Social Course for Catholic Men at the Mission Seminary, June 1961. Roma: Mission Seminary.

Ashton, H. 1967. *The Basuto: A Social Study of Traditional and Modern Lesotho*. London: Oxford University Press.

Danziger, C.A. 1979. *Traders' Century – The Fortunes of Frasers*. Cape Town: Purnell.

Du Bois, D. 2012. 'The "Coolie Curse": The Evolution of White Colonial Attitudes towards the Indian Question, 1860–1900', *Historia* 57(2): 35–37.

Ellenberger, D.F. [1912] 1992. *History of the Basuto: Ancient and Modern*. Morija: Morija Archives and Museum.

Hart, K. and V. Padayachee. 2000. 'Indian Business in South Africa after Apartheid: New and Old Trajectories', *Comparative Studies in Society* 42(4): 683–712.

Pim, A. 1935. *Financial and Economic Position of Basutoland: Report of the Commission Appointed by the Secretary of State for Dominion Affairs*. London: His Majesty's Stationery Office.

Rantheba, L. 1985. 'The History of the Indian Traders in Lesotho', BA dissertation. Roma: National University of Lesotho.

Theal, G.M. [1872] 2002. *Basutoland Records 1871–1872: Volume VI*. Roma: National Institute of Southern African Studies, University of Lesotho.

Thompson, A.C. 1961. *The Laws of Basutoland: Containing the Orders in Council, Proclamations and Notices, Volume I*. Cape Town: Cape Times Limited.

Walton, J. 1958. *Father of Kindness and Father of Horses – Ramosa le Ralipere: A History of Frasers Limited*. Morija: Morija Printing Works.

CHAPTER 4

Basotho in Colonial Commerce, 1900s–1966

Introduction

This chapter explores the experiences of early Basotho traders in colonial commerce, with a focus on their entrepreneurial pursuits against stacked odds. The colonial government issued Basotho licences to trade in the peripheral and mountainous areas outside the busy centres, and by the turn of the century, several Basotho had broken into commerce. These early Basotho traders struggled to keep their businesses afloat. As a result, many sought loans from European and Indian traders to bail them out.

Despite these loans, the early Basotho businesses failed due to the impact of the economic depression of the 1920s and 1930s. This allowed European traders to accuse the Basotho of not being business minded. From about twelve in the 1920s, there were only three Basotho in business by the mid-1930s. I demonstrate here that though Basotho worked hard to run their businesses in the newly introduced system of trading, emancipation through commerce was denied by a colonial system that worked to undermine their economic independence in order to sustain supplies of cheap labour. The government implemented a series of segregationist policies to strangulate Basotho economic pursuits; to mask these exclusionary policies, Europeans argued that the Basotho lacked modern business skills, culture and spirit.

These restrictions notwithstanding, more Basotho broke into local commerce, some trading informally without licences – particularly women. The Basotho had their breakthrough in 1951, when the administration relaxed several bureaucratic bottlenecks. Their numbers increased, Basotho traders organised themselves through co-operatives to address their problems of access to credit and supply of stock. To undermine local European wholesalers, they started procuring their business supplies directly from South African firms.

The work of the underdevelopment school has been instrumental in explaining how colonialism exploited Africa (Rodney 1972; Amin 1972). This approach became popular in the 1970s as a moral and economic critique of the 'global world system', which privileged the North at the expense of the South. Underdevelopment scholars emphasised unequal global terms of trade to show how the 'core/centre' (the North) exploited the 'periphery' (the South). A local *comprador* elite which worked for colonial interests connected the two points. Basotho chiefs fell into this category (we will see later that they were replaced by politicians after independence).

In addition, Marxist theorists attacked the neoclassical school and dependency theorists for their reductionism and focus on exchange rather than relations of production and class struggle. They asked how systems developed, functioned and changed in space and time, using the dominant analytical tools of their trade: modes of production, and dialectical and historical materialism (Zeleza 1993). Wolpe's (1972) theory of cheap labour in South Africa advanced that modes of production could 'articulate' – meaning that different systems of economic organisation can co-exist. For example, he argued that Africans used low wages earned in the capitalist mining economy of South Africa to sustain rural subsistence agriculture in least industrial economies. Wolpe participated more in the French Marxists' 'Modes of Production' debates of the 1970s. The origins of this school of thought are attributed to the works of Louis Pierre Althusser, the Algerian-born French Marxist (Freund 1985).

Both the 1970s Marxists' discussions and those of neo-Marxists, however, have neglected commerce and Africans' participation in it. This chapter will therefore explore Basotho participation in commerce, and how the Basotho sought to redefine terms between South Africa (the 'core') and Lesotho (the 'periphery').

Early Basotho Traders

From the late nineteenth century, some Basotho started picking up business skills working as European traders' clerks, salesmen and touts. In the 1870s, for instance, David Sebaka worked for a European trader called Wells. During the Gun War, Wells left Sebaka in charge of his business, leading Dr Eugène Casalis (cited in Germond 1967: 367) to remark: 'That is a fine example of honesty among our Blacks'. In 1916, the Resident Commissioner informed the High Commissioner, Viscount Gladstone, that 'European traders employ natives as clerks and salesmen'.[1] Available data suggests that the colonial government issued twelve trading licences

Table 4.1. Early Basotho traders.

Name	Year issued	Village/Area	District
1. Jos Makotoane	1906	Morija	Maseru
2. Adam Mosito	1909	Moliboea	Leribe
3. Ramakoaba	1909	Moliboea	Leribe
4. Thaane	1909	Bakeng	Leribe
5. James Putsoane	1912	Thaba-Tseka	Maseru
6. Samuel Hatla	1912	Butha-Buthe	Butha-Buthe
7. Osiel Mteane	1913	Mashai	Maseru
8. L. Lephaila	1915	Helehehle	Quthing
9. Caleb Sebatane	1919	'Meta	Quthing
10. Thomas Mofolo	1925	Bokong	Leribe
11. Rantsatsaila Kou	1925	Ribaneng	Mafeteng
12. George Kou	1935	Setleketseng	Maseru

Sources: This table was constructed from the data found in the following archival sources: *LNA, Trade, S3/26/1/6*, Assistant Commissioner's Office in Leribe to Government Secretary in Maseru, 27 February 1925; *Naleli ea Lesotho* newspaper, vol. xx1, no. 653, 24 July 1925.

to Basotho between 1906 and 1935 – nine licences between 1906 and 1919, two more between 1919 and 1925 and one in 1935.[2] Table 4.1 shows a list of these early Basotho traders.

All these early licences were issued in areas outside the busier town centres. Table 4.2 shows the number of licences across the country in 1935. The capital, Maseru, had a total of thirty-three licences, with thirty-two held by European traders and only one by a Mosotho trader, who operated in Setleketseng, a village outside the town centre.

For the most part, these Basotho ran small shops that were supported financially by European traders. Many of their stores collapsed due to financial problems during the depression of the late 1920s and early 1930s, with the exceptions of three Basotho traders – Thomas Mofolo, Rantsatsaila Kou and George Kou – who had broken into local commerce much later.[3] For example, when Samuel Hatla opened his store in 1912

Table 4.2. Trading licences in Basutoland by 1935.

District(s)	Europeans	Indians	Basotho	Total
Leribe	27	4	1	32
Butha-Buthe	10	10	—	20
Berea	23	2	—	25
Maseru	32	—	1	33
Mafeteng	25	—	1	26
Mohale's Hoek	18	—	—	18
Quthing	19	—	—	19
Qacha's Nek & Mokhotlong	21	—	—	21
Total	**175**	**16**	**3**	**194**

Sources: This table was adapted from Pim (1935: 60).

(see Table 4.1), he was financially assisted by Frasers, who also periodically gave him stock on credit, while L. Lephaila was backed by W.G. Brown.[4] Commenting on financial flows between Basotho and European traders, Pim remarked that: 'In the past credit has been given to a very considerable extent' (1935: 61).

When Basotho businesses failed, European sponsors took over their licences as payment. It was easier for more powerful actors to acquire licences in this manner, rather than going through bureaucratic red tape; indeed, for them it was a guaranteed acquisition. Moteane Brothers, for instance, owed H. & A. Payne Ltd £1,900 and James Cole £900. In February 1920, W.A. Crooks cleared their debt on condition that he took over their businesses.[5]

Taking over Basotho defaulters' licences led to some conflicts between Europeans. Marginalised, weaker member of the Chamber felt that the stronger firms deliberately sponsored Basotho, knowing that their businesses would collapse eventually, and that they would assume the licences. By then, the consensus was that Basotho businesses were bound to fail because they lacked business skills and culture. Andreas Metsing applied for a licence in 1929. In opposing his application, G.P. Higgs argued at the Licensing Board that: 'Andreas would be indirectly supported by some Europeans, which would mean that the station would eventually become the property of the European'.[6]

Europeans used this narrative about Basotho business skills to oppose Basotho applications to the Licensing Board. In a letter to the Assistant Commissioner in Leribe district, the Chamber argued that Basotho were not 'capable of running stores'.[7] Using the case of Samuel Hatla (see Table 4.1) to prove their point, the Chamber added that he 'gave a great deal of [credit] to his friends & preferred to stand & look at his stock of mealies then sell them when the market was favourable', and that 'he had to be told when the markets were favourable'.[8] The Pim Commission endorsed this observation, remarking that Basotho 'are not as a rule business like in their methods' (1935:61).

The Pim Commission arrived in October 1934. Pim was a British financial expert appointed by the Colonial Office to investigate the country's economic situation, and the Commission was financed by the Colonial Development Fund as part of a general survey of the economy in various colonies. Following the First World War, Britain sought to create an open international economic order, based on world peace and harmonisation of relations with its colonies, to ensure the Empire's self-sufficiency and lessen dependency on other countries in the North (see Hancock 1940).

The Colonial Government's Strategy of Segregation

The colonial government restricted Indian traders to the northern districts in order to protect European traders from competition. It dealt with Basotho traders in a slightly different fashion. In the twentieth century, more Basotho showed a keen interest in business and sought inclusion as traders more aggressively. It was harder for the colonial government and the Chamber to contain a newly emerging class of missionary-educated Basotho (see Chapter 5). As a result, the British took systematic steps to undermine Basotho efforts to be included in local commerce. The Basutoland Native Trading Proclamation No. 76 of 1936 and the Basotho Credit Restriction Proclamation of 1937 were passed accordingly. These two laws segregated Basotho from European and Indian traders.

The Pim Commission recommended that the Basotho be given more opportunities, especially in the lowlands. With little capital and inadequate financial support for their businesses, it was difficult for Basotho to afford the General Dealer's licence fee, and they could not repay their debts, as we have seen. The Commission recommended that the colonial government create a different licence for Basotho, admitting that '[t]he issue of trading licences to natives [is] a difficult problem … [because] their capital [is] usually inadequate' (Pim 1935: 62).

As a result, the colonial government created a Restricted Licence, or Native Trading Licence, through the Native Trading Proclamation of 1936. The licence prevented Basotho traders from selling lucrative business items such as wool, mohair, manufactured goods and livestock; instead, they could sell only small articles like groceries and stationery (Pim 1935: 60–61; Ashton 1967: 166–85; Fenton 1905: 267). The Commission claimed that '[this] business could be carried on with much less capital and in much simpler premises' (Pim 1935: 63). The government did not immediately introduce the licence, since it was not yet 'finalised to their best interests'.[9]

Instead of issuing Restricted Licences, the government created the Café Licence for Basotho through Government Notice No. 50 of 1940.[10] This new licence allowed trading in small items like candles, matches, paraffin, flour, sugar and salt, although these items were not to be sold in bulk (Mphanya 2010: 64). In 1942, however, the colonial government informed the public that it would not issue any new licences due to the impact of the Second World War.[11] Instead, it enforced Section 4 of the Native Trading Proclamation. This section prohibited Basotho from entering into any form of business partnership with European and Indian traders. They could not be financially supported by these groups or procure business supplies on credit. Many struggled to support their businesses as a result. Section 4(1) insisted:

> No person other than a native shall enter into partnership with the holder of a native trader's licence or be employed in any capacity whatsoever, other than that of an auditor in the business carried on by any native trader, nor shall any person other than a native acquire any interest whatever in any such business.[12]

To further enforce segregation, the government promulgated the Basutoland Credit Restriction Proclamation of 1937, which was to 'regulate and restrict the grant of credit to natives living in Basutoland'.[13] As with the Native Trading Proclamation, Pim had advised that the colonial government must take measures to protect European traders' from Basotho defaulters. Due to the economic hardships of recent decades, many Basotho could not settle their debts. European traders complained to the Commission that: 'Basuto used formerly to do their best to repay such debts … their honesty in this respect [has] greatly diminished' (Pim 1935: 61).

Worse, European traders could not recover their debts legally because of the dual judicial system. Civil cases involving Basotho debtors were handled through customary courts as opposed to colonial magistrate courts. Even if Europeans used colonial courts, a chief had still to be consulted, and in the European traders' view, the chiefs did not put any pressure on the debtor to pay.[14] In 1937, the *Mochochonono* newspaper reported European traders' debt grievances against the Basotho: 'In Basutoland when credit is given it is not easy to recover owing to the dual system of rule. There are European courts and native courts in which cases against Natives could be brought for the recovery of debt'. It was difficult for them to recover their money because according to 'Native custom a debtor is not pressed to pay his debt, while according to European courts before the writ could be executed the chief of the Native concerned must be consulted'.[15]

The 1951 Breakthrough

The colonial government finally implemented the Native Trading Proclamation of 1936 when it passed Proclamation No. 72 of 1951.[16] It would issue a Restricted Licence to a prospective trader when they proved, by a bank statement, assets or cash, that they had capital ranging between £250 and £350. Livestock were not taken as assets because the government argued that they were not easily converted to cash. The government sought to promote a national currency as the dominant form of money at the expense of any other form; it had begun this process in the 1870s when it enforced that the Hut Tax must be paid in cash only. A Café Licence could be upgraded to a Restricted Licence, to allow the holder to expand their business activities –on limited scale, of course. If a trader was operating a successful café, they could be evaluated by the Licensing Board and then upgraded to a Restricted Licence with additional capital of £200–£300.[17]

By the mid-1950s, more Basotho had acquired traders' licences. Those who took advantage of the relaxation of colonial laws tended to be South African mine workers, civil servants and teachers (Mphanya 2010: 63), while many Second World War veterans invested their gratuities in retail stores upon their return.[18] Basotho mostly adopted a plural approach to their economic activities. Business was an addition to their agriculture, hawking, wage employment, informal trade, livestock trading and selling of handicrafts. Those with large livestock holdings also sold wool and mohair to European traders, who in turn exported to international markets.

In Leribe, the number of Restricted Licences increased from seventy-five in 1951 to 118 in 1954. In the same district, Café Licences owned by Basotho traders outside the town centre amounted to 218, but there were only ten Basotho-owned cafés inside the town centre. In Maseru, there were 300 Basotho-owned Café Licences in the same year.[19] The Colonial Office commented that: 'Although European and Indian Traders still predominate, African interest in trading is steadily increasing and Basuto-held trading licences are likely soon to exceed those held by non-Basuto' (British Information Services 1952: 70).

The 1951 Proclamation introduced another important change: it allowed more Basotho women to break into local commerce. Basotho women did not previously qualify for a licence because the colonial government had exempted them from paying tax under the Native Tax Proclamation No. 3 of 1911.[20] Taxation was the primary means to force men, and not women, to work in the mines, but its payment was required when applying for a trading licence. In 1940, the Basutoland Native Trading Proclamation of 1936 was amended by Proclamation No. 64 to lift the tax prerequisites for women. The Proclamation defined eligible women as 'any member of an African tribal race living in the Territory whose father or husband was or is domiciled and paid or pays native tax'.[21]

From 1951, several Basotho women were issued a trader's licence – either a Café Licence or a Restricted Licence – to open stores. However, even though colonial law allowed them to apply for traders' licences, only a few women owned stores before independence. Most Basotho traders were men: in 1951, for example, there were seventy-five Restricted Licences in the Leribe District issued to Basotho in places outside the town centre. Out of that total, eleven were owned by women. In April 1953, out of twenty-four traders' licence applications in the same district, six applications were made by women. Five of them were successful.[22]

Basotho women had not remained passive observers in the economy before the Native Trading Proclamation. They participated in local trade as informal business owners, producing and selling handicrafts, ornaments, food, traditional beer, grain, legumes, vegetables and similar products. They used their profits, savings and remittances to apply for trading licences. In some cases, working husbands launched their wives or sisters into business.

Thibella is south-east of Maseru central, located near Lesotho's mineworkers' agency, the Native Recruiting Corporation. This area was famous for beer houses (*shebeens*), which were said to prevent ('*thibella*') miners from reaching home since they spent all their money on beer and women. One of the locally prominent businesswomen in this area was Polo Thajane, popularly known as 'Mamak'hanakisi – a name she acquired from the delicious spicy food she served. She sold home-brewed beer and food and ran a butcher's shop, as well as a delivery business using a horse and cart. She moved to a different location out of town in the 1940s, where she ran her businesses with her daughters and granddaughters until she died in 1969 (Ambrose 1993: 159–60).

Mining remittances were never adequate for the sustenance of families back home. Worse, there were men – called *Makholoa* – who left their families and married new wives in South Africa, or squandered their money abroad promiscuously. Some came back after many years, while others stayed away or supported multiple families. As a result, the everyday burden of supporting a domestic unit of extended family members rested squarely with women.

In 1958, the government estimated that there were 2,700 Basotho licence holders countrywide. These were in the categories of Restricted Licences, cafés, bakeries, butcheries, livestock trading, milling and transport. Access to a General Dealers' Licence, however, continued to be monopolised by European traders.[23] It is not surprising that as late as 1964 – two years before independence – the colonial government observed that '[t]he bulk of the general trade in the Territory is carried on by Europeans and also, in the northern districts, by a few Indians'.[24]

The Rise of the Co-operative Movement

Though more Basotho broke into local commercial circles after 1951, many continued to have difficulties accessing credit from the banks and procuring stock for their businesses. Colonial financial institutions were not geared towards advancing Basotho business interests. Private investors and the colonial government established several financial institutions to support the newly emergent labour-reserve economy controlled by European traders. In 1891, the Basutoland Post Office Savings Bank was established to facilitate flows of money and information between Lesotho and South Africa. Its deposits were passed on to the South African Post Office Bank (Thabane 2009: 4).

In 1862, a British bank, Standard Bank, established a branch in the Cape, and by September 1901, it was advertising its banking services in Basutoland. In the beginning, it operated as an agency managed by Alfred Ellenberger, who would travel on horseback between Lesotho and Ladybrand in the Free State to make deposits and withdrawals. In 1904, Standard Bank established a branch in Maseru (Ambrose 1993: 91). Around this time, the Bloemfontein Board of Executives and Trust Company, an insurance company, also opened a branch in Maseru, although it stopped its operations in 1932 during the Great Depression when it went bankrupt. Other Cape-based insurance companies, like Mutual Building Homes Limited, also started to advertise their services in Basutoland (Thabane 2009: 3–4).

Commercial banks presented themselves as 'saving institutions' and not 'lenders of credit', particularly to Basotho. This could be seen in how they advertised their services. For instance, when Standard Bank opened a branch in Maseru, it advertised that it had done so for 'the purpose of all transactions/operations carried out by banks, that is, to receive and save money in its interest' (Thabane 2009: 6). Similarly, the Post Office Savings Bank advertised: 'If you are paid in cash, you have to save it for the COMING DAYS. Go to the Post Office near you, they will tell you how you can get a savings book and you can start saving' (ibid.: 6–7).

These financial institutions predominantly served a white clientele of civil servants, missionaries and European traders. Basotho established alternative savings and farmers' co-operatives, with assistance from Christian missionaries. These co-operatives dealt with the economic hardship faced by Basotho. Part of the money earned from wages and the sale of produce or livestock was invested in the co-operatives, as well as in agriculture and small enterprises. Various co-operatives kept their monies with commercial banks. Their members would pool their money in order to procure farm implements and groceries, as well as providing credit to members (Pim 1935: 172–73).

The co-operative movement flourished quickly because of the pre-existence of Basotho communal work parties (*matsema*) and extended families. This spirit of social interdependence led the Pim Commission to comment that: 'The conception of co-operation is by no means foreign to life under tribal conditions in which a practical working communism is a striking feature'. The Commission added: 'The native family, in the large sense of that term, may almost be described as a readymade co-operative' (Pim 1935: 174).

Despite the enthusiasm for them, however, many early co-operatives failed. Some that survived were handicapped by members defaulting on their debts. For example, in 1938, the African Co-operative Society loaned money to all its members with financial difficulties. About £380 of the £880 credit issued to members never returned. The Pim Commission recommended that the government should not encourage the development of co-operatives because they were regarded as having achieved their aims as soon as they received assistance from donors. Even so, Basotho continued to form co-operatives, and the colonial government was forced to pass Proclamation No. 47 of 1948 to officially recognise and control them (Thompson 1961: 2056–58).

From the 1950s, the co-operative movement became critical for Basotho traders' attempts to strengthen their presence in local business. By the middle of that decade, nationalist sentiment had gripped the country, and it was generally accepted that independence for the Basotho and their country was merely a matter of time. After years of supporting European traders, the colonial government was eager to increase local participation in an economy that was soon to be handed over to a Lesotho government. It was now willing to assist Basotho traders and other formations in their attempts to gain control of the local economy, including the formation of co-operatives.

In December 1957, the colonial government helped establish the Basutoland Co-operative Banking Union (BCBU, later just the Banking Union) under the Registrar of Co-operatives (Mphanya 2004). This new co-operative bank collected deposits and provided credit to its members. It could give its members credit because the government had agreed to guarantee its loans from commercial banks; with the borrowed money, the Banking Union advanced loans to its members (Thabane 1998: 10). It also had a Wholesale department where its members bought stock for their businesses. This institution operated for about five years, but in 1963, the Registrar of Co-operatives reported that it was 'totally bankrupt and beyond recovery'.[25] It was liquidated as a result.

Major factors leading to its collapse were poor repayment of loans by its members and failure to cope with the high interest rates it paid on loans from commercial banks (Morse 1960: 245–46). A Commission of Inquiry investigating the collapse of Coop Lesotho some years later added that the collapse of the Banking Union was brought about by imprudent investment in the construction of a two-storey building, Bonhomme House, in Maseru, which drained the co-operative's liquidity. In the report on the bank's closure, final accounts demonstrated that it had an overall deficit of almost R330,000. More than 50 per cent of all its funds and credit from commercial banks had not been recovered.[26]

In October 1963, the government registered a new co-operative, the Finance and Marketing Co-operative Union of Basutoland Ltd (FMCUB), known for short as the Co-operative Union of Basutoland (CUB). All the assets belonging to the Banking Union were transferred to the Co-operative Union, which operated like a commercial bank, providing loans against 100 per cent security (*Basutoland Times*, 1 November 1963: 1–4).

Summary

From the beginning of the twentieth century, the Basotho pragmatically inserted themselves into the exclusive local economy. Moving beyond agricultural production, they invested their money in commerce. Through an array of plural and collective economic activities, they organised themselves to expand the restrictions of commerce and finance, and in doing so they emphasised mutuality and solidarity, traits that had declined by the end of the nineteenth century.

We have seen in this chapter a mutation of traditional Basotho cultural practices of collectivism (exemplified by work parties, or *matsema*), now adapted to support commercial activity. (This spirit of collectivism had played a fundamental role in the rise of the Basotho nation earlier on – see Chapter 1.) This fuelled the rise of the co-operative movement, forcing the government to bureaucratically recognise Basotho initiatives. In this way, the Basotho undermined the stereotypes of economic individualism dominant in capitalism and underpinning colonial commerce. At the same time, they did not reject the pursuit of profit and wealth accumulation. Instead, we witness an ontological point of difference that blends individual interests with mutual solidarity to create a more inclusive economy.

NOTES

Part of the material in this chapter was originally published in *HISTORIA* and the copyrights of this specific content format belong to the Historical Association of South Africa.

1. *LNA, Indian Immigration, S3/14/1/2*, Resident Commissioner to High Commissioner, South Africa, 1916.
2. *LNA, Trade, S3/26/1/6*, Assistant Commissioner's Office in Leribe to Government Secretary in Maseru, 27 February 1925.
3. *LNA, Trade, S3/26/1/8–11*, Letters of the Basutoland Chamber of Commerce, and those of its individual members, to the Resident Commissioner, Maseru, 1927–32.
4. *LNA, Trade, S3/26/1/6*, Basutoland Chamber of Commerce to Assistant Commissioner, Quthing, 25 July 1924.
5. *LNA, Trade, S3/26/1/6*, Assistant Commissioner's Office in Leribe to the Government Secretary, Maseru, 27 February 1925.
6. *LNA, Trade, S3/26/1/10*, G.P. Higgs to the Licensing Meeting, Leribe, 9 December 1929.
7. *LNA, Trade, S3/26/1/6*, Basutoland Chamber of Commerce to the Assistant Commissioner, Leribe, 30 July 1924.
8. *LNA, Trade, S3/26/1/6*, Basutoland Chamber of Commerce to the Assistant Commissioner, Botha-Bothe, 25 July 1924.

9. *NULA, Trade, LC 23/3.*
10. *NULA, Trade, LC 23/1*, Government Circular No. 47 of 1953 to all District Commissioners, 9 October 1953.
11. *NULA, Trade, LC3/5*, Government Circular No. 27 of 1945 to all District Commissioners, Maseru, 9 October 1953. This notice was repealed in 1953 by Circular No. 47 of 1953.
12. *NULA, Trade, LC 23/3.*
13. Proclamation No. 8 of 1937, *Basutoland Proclamations and Notices, 1937.*
14. Basutoland Credit Restriction Proclamation, an official summary in *Mochochonono*, vol. xxvii, no. 1282, 13 March 1937, 7.
15. Ibid.
16. *Basutoland Proclamations and Notices, 1951.*
17. *NULA, Trade, LC 23/3*, Government Circular No. 25 of 1952 to all District Commissioners, 10 April 1952.
18. *Basutoland Colonial Annual Reports, 1947*, 28.
19. *NULA, Trade, LC 23/11*, Government Secretary in Maseru to all District Commissioners, 28 May 1954.
20. The Proclamation allowed only men to pay tax: *Basutoland Proclamations and Notices, 1911.*
21. *Basutoland Proclamations and Notices, 1940.*
22. *NULA, Trade, LC 23/1*, Office of the District Commissioner in Leribe to the Government Secretary in Maseru, 15 April 1953.
23. *LNA, Basutoland Colonial Annual Reports, 1958*, 45.
24. *LNA, Basutoland Colonial Annual Reports, 1964*, 37.
25. Summary of the Report of BCBU Liquidation, *Basutoland Times*, no. 45, 8 November 1963, 1–4.
26. Ibid.

REFERENCES

Ambrose, D. 1993. *Illustrated History of Maseru.* Morija: Morija Museum and Archives.

Amin, S. 1972. 'Underdevelopment and Dependence in Africa – Origins and Contemporary Forms', *Journal of Modern African Studies* 10(4): 503–24.

Ashton, H. 1967. *The Basuto: A Social Study of Traditional and Modern Lesotho.* London: Oxford University Press.

British Information Services. 1952. *An Economic Survey of the Colonial Territories (1951): Volume I: The Central African and High Commission Territories – Northern Rhodesia, Nyasaland, Basutoland, Bechunaland, and Swaziland.* London: His Majesty's Stationery Office.

Fenton, R. 1905. *Peculiar People in a Pleasant Land: A South African Narrative.* Pretoria: Pretoria Publishing Company.

Freund, B. 1985. 'The Modes of Production Debate in African Studies', *Canadian Journal of African Studies* 19(1): 23–29.

Germond, R.C. 1967. *Chronicles of Basutoland: A Running Commentary on the Events of the Years 1830–1902 by the French Protestant Missionaries in Southern Africa*. Morija: Morija Sesuto Book Depot.

Hancock, W.K. 1940. *Survey of British Commonwealth Affairs Volume II: Problems of Economic Policy, 1918–1939, Part 1*. London: Oxford University Press.

Morse, C. 1960. *Basutoland, Bechuanaland Protectorate and Swaziland: Report of an Economic Survey Mission*. London: Her Majesty's Stationery Office.

Mphanya, N. 2004. *A Brief History of Basutoland Congress Party, Lekhotla la Mahatam-moho: 1952–2002*. Morija: Morija Printing Works.

———. 2010. *My Life in the Basutoland Congress Party*. Maseru: Motjoli Publishers.

Pim, A. 1935. *Financial and Economic Position of Basutoland: Report of the Commission Appointed by the Secretary of State for Dominion Affairs*. London: His Majesty's Stationery Office.

Rodney, W. 1972. *How Europe Underdeveloped Africa*. London: Bogle-L'Ouvertune Publications.

Thabane, M. 1998. 'Financial Institutions in the Destruction of the Natural Economy and Attempts at Capitalist Developments in Lesotho', *Nordic Africa Institute Conference on Financial Institutions in the Political Economy: Cases Studies from Pre-colonial, Colonial and Post-Colonial Africa*. Rosendal, 11–14 June 1998. Norway: Nordic Africa Institute.

———. 2009. 'Indigenous Entrepreneurial Initiative and Attempts to Solve Problems of Access to Credit in Lesotho, 1868–1975', *Historical Studies Seminar Series*, Roma, 11 September 2009. Roma: Department of Historical Studies, National University of Lesotho.

Thompson, A.C. 1961. *The Laws of Basutoland: Containing the Orders in Council, Proclamations and Notices, Volume I*. Cape Town: Cape Times Limited.

Wolpe, H. 1972. 'Capitalism and Cheap Labour-Power in South Africa: From Segregation to Apartheid', *Economy and Society* 1(4): 425–54.

Zeleza, P.T. 1993. *A Modern Economic History of Africa, Vol. 1: The Nineteenth Century*. Nairobi: East African Educational Publishers Ltd.

CHAPTER 5

The Political Struggle for Reform of Trade, 1900s–1966

Introduction

Economic pragmatism could only take the Basotho so far. I advance here that they also fought politically to confront the injustices of the colonial economy, by seeking reform of commerce and their inclusion in a country they believed belonged to them. Europeans' control of local commerce fed the rise of the national liberation struggle for independence, as part of the anti-colonial movement worldwide. The European monopoly defined commerce as a landscape of contestation. Now with ideas instead of guns, the Basotho fought for justice.

By the turn of the century, missionary education and the labour-migration system had produced new social groups within Basotho society; from these, the vanguards of the liberation struggle emerged. In South African mines, cities and institutions of higher learning, Basotho interacted with other African groups in similar predicaments. These new groups, with their exposure to urban politics and conditions, launched a revolution. By this point the Basotho were already battling with the colonial authorities, chiefs and European traders for reform and political and economic inclusion.

The organisations involved in this battle were the Basutoland Progressive Association, the League of Commoners, the League of Justice and the Basotho Traders' Association. These early political movements birthed political parties. In the historiography of Lesotho, the social and political activism of these organisations in the liberation struggle is well documented (Edgar 1987; Machobane 1990; Nyeko 2002a; Weisfelder 1974, 1999). Little is written about the economic side of their struggle, particularly activism around the reformation of commerce and Basotho inclusion therein.

Poverty and Inequality Deepen

The collapse of Basotho economic prosperity, their exclusion from colonial commerce and their dependence on low wages ensured that poverty and inequality deepened across the country. The chiefs grew rich and powerful under the colonial system of indirect rule, and benefitted the most from tax enforcement and the privatised labour-recruitment system. The chiefs also charged people in their courts and issued punitive fines; they demanded more livestock from the people and labour in their fields. By the 1930s, court fines were mostly paid in cash, which went into their pockets as tribute. Finally, the chiefs obliged people to participate in communal work parties for commercial purposes (Ashton 1967: 220; Leys 1981: 90–91).

The Pim Commission carried out a survey of inequality in the district of Qacha's Nek in 1934. This revealed that about 80 per cent of those who had been paying tax for the last five to ten years had no livestock (Pim 1935). In 1936, the colonial government surveyed the Highlands region; a sample showed that 11 per cent of the people had around twenty head of cattle, while 50 per cent only had small livestock and the rest had nothing. A wealthy group of principal chiefs, village headmen and a few favoured commoners[1] owned extensive tracts of land and stock. Their lavish lifestyle included tailored suits, cars and capital-intensive farming equipment, and their children were educated in advanced missionary schools (Leys 1981: 91). An observer reported that:

> In 1934, one chief, who kindly showed me his books, owned 200 cattle, 1,500 small stock, 90 equines, and 31 large lands, which in a fair year yielded 300 bags of grain; he had also a revenue from his court of about 200 cattle, 225 small stock and 20 pounds cash, and an allowance of 100 pounds (subsequently raised to 300 pounds) from the administration. He was one of the wealthier chiefs, but not as wealthy as the late Chief Jonathan, who died leaving an estate worth over 20,000 pounds. (Cited in ibid.)

In contrast, the majority of Basotho had little or nothing. They had no livestock and could not feed, clothe or house themselves adequately (ibid.). With limited economic opportunities, increasing population and exclusion from commerce, the Basotho had no option but to fight for their inclusion through reform of colonial trade.

The Basutoland Progressive Association

In 1904, a group of missionary-educated teachers began informal discussions about the deteriorated economic position of the Basotho. In 1907, they officially launched the Basutoland Progressive Association under the leadership of Reverend Crammer Sebeta and Simon Phamotse. The Association's members belonged to an emergent elite of commoners, locally known as the 'Intelligentsia' (Bahlalefi) or 'Progressives' (Matsoelopele).

Most of these were PEMS missionary-educated teachers, writers, government clerks, interpreters, ministers of religion and businessmen (Gill 1993: 170).

Using Western education and Eurocentric development ideals, the Progressive Association's aims were to eliminate racial discrimination, increase commoners' representation in the National Council, check the chiefs' abuse of power, modernise agriculture, promote the improvement of social services and assist in creating small-scale industries.[2]

> For the educated Protestant elite that dominated the Progressive Association, progress meant attaining some of the benefits from western technology [in addition to] restructuring traditional Basotho political institutions and values to conform more closely to the British model of parliamentary democracy … [For them], progress was also thought to imply moderation, restraint, and the tactics of "gentle persuasion" in order to demonstrate that Basotho were not backward savages but a people that could gradually assume broad political responsibilities. (Weisfelder 1974: 398)

Licencing Board meetings and newspaper columns became battlegrounds where Basotho traders met their European and Indian counterparts. Writing with specific reference to the Licencing Board meetings that sat in 1925 to consider the applications of Rantsatsaila Kou and Thomas Mofolo, one Mosotho columnist in the *Naleli ea Lesotho* newspaper reported:

> The jobs which Basotho are still attempting here in Lesotho now are not the ones which it appears as if they are conflicting with the whites; but this one of business, it is the one that a white person fights with a Mosotho, you could actually see that this Lesotho no longer belongs to Basotho in terms of business, it now belongs to the whites. Even the Paramount Chief, they no longer see him as anything … It is not right when the development brought by white traders here in Lesotho leads to hatred of a Mosotho, the owner of the country. Mafeteng here … an applicant was one, it was Mr. Kou only, but the councils which were fighting over the application were in two parts. It was the one of the white traders fighting the application of Mr. Kou saying that he would destroy their business, he would block them. They were really fighting with strength. The black ones were … saying that Kou should be given that place. (*Naleli ea Lesotho,* vol. xx1, no. 653, 25 July 1925. Translated from Sesotho)

Apart from supporting Basotho licence applications, the Association actively participated in the Licencing Board meetings to oppose various applications from European and Indian traders. In June 1927, for instance, Thomas Mofolo and Simon Phamotse – as delegates of the association – attended a Licencing Board meeting in the district of Qacha's Nek to oppose one Indian trader from opening a trading station. Mofolo pointed out that the applicant should not be granted a traders' licence in the district because he already had five stations elsewhere. He argued that 'Indians [were] not an asset to the country [because] … their money goes to India and their food comes from India'. Therefore, 'they will do nothing but harm'.[3] He also stressed that they imported other Indians to do their work instead of employing Basotho.[4]

Often, both European and Basotho traders shared strong anti-Indian sentiments and used racial and nationalistic assertions to oppose Indians in the Board sittings. On this occasion, the Indian trader's application was rejected. He appealed the outcome, arguing that 'the grounds of opposition relied on by the Native Progressive Association … that Indians do not employ Basuto should not be a reason for withholding a Licence'.[5] In spite of this attempt, his appeal failed.

On a different occasion, the Progressive Association successfully opposed two applications lodged by European traders. In November 1935, it wrote a letter of protest to the Assistant Commissioner in Teyateyaneng arguing that the European traders should not be given a licence to trade in the town. As a result of this intervention, the two European applicants were not granted trading licences in the district's town centre. The Association wrote:

> As a committee of Basutoland Progressive Association, we feel justified in lodging a strong protest against these two applications in the interest of the native community of Basutoland on the grounds that all the Trading stores in the camp (town centre) belong to Europeans … Basutoland being the only place where the Basuto have rights of trading, therefore we wish that new Licences should be granted to Basuto only.[6]

Despite its persistence, the Association was not always successful in opposing the issue of new licences. It was virtually impossible to win against economic giants such as Frasers. In 1935, Frasers was awarded two licences to open stations in the villages of Marakabei and 'Maletsunyane in the central highlands, despite opposition from the Association (*Mochochonono Newspaper*, 7 December 1935: 7). From the 1950s and 1960s, Europeans expanded into the mountain areas, where the Basotho had large flocks of small livestock. The European traders profited from supplies of wool, mohair, grain and livestock in these areas. Ashley Thorn, from one of the few remaining European trading families in Lesotho, said the following in an interview:

> [My father] bought [a store in] Thaba-Tseka in 1961 and there was no road to Thaba-Tseka ... But that was the life of a trader. I mean, each time you wanted to get further into the mountains – where the wealth was. The

farmers had big flocks of sheep and cattle and that was where the money was; wool and mohair, the buying of grain and produce.[7]

The League of Commoners (Lekhotla la Bafo)

Missionary-educated groups fought for the inclusion of Basotho in colonial commerce, but matters heated up further once the rural masses were mobilised by the League of Commoners (Lekhotla la Bafo). Its point of departure was different: with an unapologetically anticolonial line and an aggressive approach, it rejected colonial laws, European traders and the hegemonic role of the Chamber of Commerce. Its platform was a return to precolonial political, social and economic formations, with no interference from British colonial officials. The League launched a mass movement against colonial rule and successfully mobilised the rural masses.

The League proactively participated in the activities of the African National Congress, which had just been formed in 1912, in Bloemfontein. The Land Act of 1913, along with activism in the 1920s against the passes that Africans had to carry, brought Basotho and other Africans together in South Africa. The Land Act sealed the deal; it was one of the last measures meant to dismantle Africans' economic independence and to confirm them as sources of cheap labour. The Act halted sharecropping between Basotho and Afrikaners, and also ended the residence of various Basotho groups in the Orange Free State, forcing them to move back into Basutoland with its newly established borders (Murray 1981: 22–23).

The League was established by the Lefela brothers and their associates in 1919. The oldest brother, Josiel Lefela – born around 1885 – was the most influential in its formation and activities. His younger brother, Maphutseng Lefela (born around 1895) was more educated, having reached high-school level at Lovedale in the Eastern Cape. Before becoming the secretary general of the association, he taught in Catholic schools. Maphutseng was a 'well-read man, [and] supplied much of the intellectual firepower for the group' (Edgar 1987: 7).

Josiel had only completed three years of elementary school. He worked in the South African mines and later moved to Bechuanaland (Botswana) to become a policeman, before returning to his home in Mapoteng to operate an eating house and butchery, hawk goods in the mountains, farm, and practise as a traditional healer with initiation and circumcision schools. He became secretary and adviser to his local chief, Peete. This role launched him into national politics. 'He was well versed in traditional law and chiefs from around Mapoteng often called on him for advice in their courts', and to 'observe cases in the District Commissioner's court in Teyateyaneng' (Edgar 1987: 7). Chief Peete held him in high esteem and had him appointed to the National Council in 1916.

As a member of the National Council, Josiel argued that the 'commoners' voices … [were] being totally neglected'. He accused the 'chiefs of cutting themselves off from the ordinary Basotho and abusing their positions' through the Council (Nyeko 2002a: 140). His activism was informed by first-hand participant observation. As an alternative to the National Council, he proposed the formation of a Council of Commoners. This, he believed, would be an important democratic alternative for ordinary Basotho. His proposal was rejected by the Council and Paramount Chief Griffith; as a result, Josiel formed the League of Commoners in 1919 (ibid.).

The Paramount Chief wanted to expel Josiel from the National Council with immediate effect, but the Resident Commissioner, E.F. Garaway, warned against such a swift move. Josiel was loved by the people and expelling him could be a disaster for the government. Garaway soon abandoned this tolerant stance and expelled Josiel in November 1920, after Josiel published an article in the *Naleli* newspaper in the September of that year entitled: 'How Shall We Do Away with the Black Race?' The article exposed the Europeans' 'covert and overt plans' to wipe out the blacks (Edgar 1987: 9). The gist of the article was as follows:

> For a long time the Europeans in South Africa have been considering and asking themselves how they can stop the increase of the blacks who are increasing while the Bushmen, owners of the land have disappeared; many plans for the ending of the black man in South Africa have been thought of; of those that have been tried many have come to grief on the way and have not reached maturity. Today, a deep scheme has been found, which anyone who does not look into clearly seems to be kindness, rather than the destruction of the whole black race in South Africa. With deep design the missionaries have been instructed to encourage everywhere the founding of Young Women's Associations. These Y.W.C.A. are to be encouraged everywhere, especially to protect against those customs which they say are sinful. Today in those associations women and girls are encouraged to collect money for building a home for Christians, young and old, to whore in. That is the way that our people will be put an end to. (Cited in ibid.: 68–69)

Consistent with its ideology, the League fought for Basotho to be allowed to trade without any need for trading licences, as was the case before colonial rule. When the government rejected many Basotho applications, the applicants continued to trade without licences. They were then arrested and prevented from trading.[8]

In 1924, the League wrote a petition to the recently appointed Resident Commissioner, J.H. Sims, the Assistant Commissioner of the organisation's home district of Berea, the Paramount Chief, and all principal chiefs, sarcastically asking them to provide 'information on the point when and how did Basuto come under the obligation of trading with licences'. It added: 'the fact remains that Basuto traded amongst themselves but they were not guilty'.[9] In the League's view, 'Basuto continued to trade without licences because they were not bound to pay for licences'.[10] As expected, the colonial government and the chiefs ignored this petition. The organisation persisted and sent a petition to the High Commissioner in Cape Town in 1927, arguing that 'the Cape Colonial laws are applied to Basuto people to put a disability on them'. They pleaded: 'Your Excellency, it is with respect and humbleness that we beg you on behalf of the Basuto nation as a whole to have mercy to allow Basuto people to trade under Sesuto customs'.[11]

This request also fell on deaf ears, and the League grew more and more angered by the colonial authorities. In August 1929, it held a meeting in the capital, Maseru. 'The Chamber of Commerce is formed for the purpose of prohibiting us from doing any trade in our country', Josiel asserted, adding that the 'aim of [the colonial government is] to abolish our nation'.[12] The League's position was that the chiefs could not act to protect their people because they 'have been bought' (Maphutseng Lefela, as cited in Edgar 1987: 139). Maphutseng added that: 'The chiefs are now completely enmeshed into the network of political and legal intrigues and are not anything but titulors [*sic*] and puppets and agents of oppression of their people in the interests of their enslaving masters' (ibid).

The League of Justice (Lekhotla la Toka)

A breakaway organisation split with the League in 1925, though it remained small, less active and less popular than its parent. This was the League of Justice (Lekhotla la Toka). Like the parent body, its stronghold was in Mapoteng, Teyateyaneng. Its members, and its leader, Justice Malitsane Mphaya Ratšiu, disagreed with the League of Commoners' position on chieftainship. Ratšiu had increasingly become critical of the influential role played by some of the chiefs within the organisation. 'While Lefela wanted chieftainship retained and restored to its pre-colonial form', Ratšiu 'felt that the chiefs were not worthy of salvaging and that the chieftainship as an institution should be abolished altogether' (Nyeko 2002a: 148).

Furthermore, while Josiel was sympathetic to the office of the Resident Commissioner and to the chiefs, but rejected all colonial officials and missionaries, Ratšiu was radically against chiefs, but in favour of missionaries and modern government institutions. Ratšiu was also an interpreter in the colonial judicial system. However, this did not place him with the BPA, which sought to modernise various traditional institutions.

One of the League of Justice's high moments was when its 'members rode horses from Mapoteng to Matsieng to tell Chieftainess 'Mantšebo to abdicate' (Nyeko 2002a: 148). Its position was that hereditary chieftainship was a colonial invention; even Moshoeshoe rose to power on his merits. Despite ideological differences between the two leaders, the organisations continued to work together; but the League of Justice fizzled out in the mid-1940s and Ratšiu returned to the League of Commoners (ibid.).

The Basuto Traders Association

In the early 1940s, Basotho traders had increased in numbers, and by 1945 they had formed their own association, the Basuto Traders Association, BTA (*Mochochonono Newspaper*, 27 October 1945: 1). This organisation provided a platform for Basotho to advance their interests in local business, while broadening the nationalist activities of earlier political organisations. There is little information on the history and activities of this association during its active years, from the 1940s to the 1960s.

Despite this, we know that it advocated for the inclusion of Basotho in colonial trade and major decision-making institutions. The Pim Commission did not find any Basotho traders' association in the mid-1930s; therefore, we know that the Basuto Traders Association was formed after that, and before 1945, when we first come across its committee. W. Mafoso was its Chairman, E.J. Malakane was the Treasurer and E.N. Tlale the Secretary. Other members of the committee were E. Lebocla and Ntsie M. Tlale, while non-committee members included popular and influential Basotho traders like Ben Mofolo, a trader from Teyateyaneng who represented all traders in the National Council.[13]

The Association represented all Basotho traders across the country, but had branches in four districts: Maseru, Mafeteng, Leribe and Berea. These are all in the western urbanised lowlands of the country. The government allowed these branches of the Association to have representatives in District Councils. In the late 1940s and 1950s, Basotho traders demanded representation on the Licensing Board – a prerogative hitherto accorded only to the (European) Chamber of Commerce. These demands were met by a united front from the Europeans and the colonial government.[14] Despite the little we know about this association, it is clear that together with other organisations, they fought for the inclusion of Basotho in commercial activities and put pressure on the colonial administration to reform colonial commerce.

The National Independence Movement

The development activities and political resistance of the Basutoland Progressive Association, the League of Commoners, the League of Justice and the Basuto Traders Association were the matrix of the twentieth-century liberation struggle. Taking over from these organisations, political parties were formed in the 1950s as the vanguard of the independence movement. Coming out first, with all guns blazing, was the Basutoland African Congress (BAC), formed in 1952 and later called the Basutoland Congress Party (BCP). This was followed by the Basutoland National Party (BNP) in 1957, and the Marematlou Freedom Party (MFP) and the Communist Party, both formed in 1962. The country's liberation struggle emphasised national independence from the British rule, resistance to incorporation into South Africa and the need to realise the Basotho's economic independence by reclaiming the local economy from the Europeans.

Born in December 1918, the charismatic Ntsu Mokhehle became a member of the League of Commoners in the 1930s, before moving to South Africa to pursue his post-primary studies at the University of Fort Hare. While there, he became a member of the African National Congress Youth League (ANCYL). He immediately identified with its revolutionary consciousness and pan-Africanist ideological predispositions. Mokhehle associated closely with the likes of Nelson Mandela and Robert Sobukwe, leading to his expulsion from the University in 1942, although he was able to finish his MSc in Zoology after being reinstated in 1944 (Matlosa and Sello 2005: 18–19).

Mokhehle taught in South Africa before returning to Lesotho in the early 1950s. Back home, the news of his political insubordination and disobedience to the colonial government and beyond had become well known. Not surprisingly, colonial administrators persistently hassled him, to the point that he could not secure a position worthy of his qualifications; instead, he became a lower-rank teacher at the Basutoland High School (Matlosa and Sello 2005: 18–19).

At the Bloemfontein Conference of 1949, the African National Congress passed a resolution stating that members coming from other countries in the region must establish African Congress branches as a strategy to mobilise the entire region. Mokhehle answered this call in 1952 when he established the Basutoland African Congress. The same year, he became the President of the Basutoland African National Teachers' Association (BANTA). BANTA was established in 1947 as a merger between the Basutoland African Teachers' Union (BATU) and the Basutoland Catholic Teachers' Association (BCTA). Responding to injustices inherent in the colonial education system, Basotho teachers formed BATU in 1943 as a non-secretariat organisation modelled on the radical Transvaal African Teachers' Union (TATU) in South Africa. In reprisal, the colonial government and the Roman Catholic Church supported the formation of a less threatening organisation, the Basutoland Catholics Teachers' Association (Nyeko 2002b: 156).

The new branch of the African Congress in Basutoland kick-started its campaign – 'self-rule at once' – by mobilising people across the country. Its political slogan was '*Ea lla koto, ea khutla nala*' – literally, 'through the wrath of a knobkerrie, our country will return'. The Congress vowed to fight for the return of Basotho lands in the Free State. Drawing on the example of the League of Commoners, and taking inspiration from its parent body in South Africa, it went beyond the Progressive Association's involvement of urban elites, workers and traders, instead building a broad united front of Basotho and bringing together the 'chiefs and commoners, Protestants and Catholics, [and] workers and peasants' (Gill 1993: 210).

Mokhehle boosted his pan-Africanist credentials by forming relations with influential African leaders, such as Kwame Nkrumah of Ghana and Abdel Nasser of Egypt. The Congress' campaigns in Basutoland gained traction after it launched its radical and anti-colonial newspaper, *The Warrior* (*Mohlabani*), in September 1954, under the editorship of Bennet Makalo Khaketla. Mokhehle and Khaketla were later expelled from the Basutoland High School on the grounds that their political activism diverted them from their teaching responsibilities (Nyeko 2002b: 159–60). In 1959, the party's name was changed to the Basutoland Congress Party (hereafter just the Congress Party).

Conservative factions in the Congress Party grew more and more agitated by its aggressive approach, with the dominant factions of the chiefs, European traders and the Catholic Church at the forefront. For some time, the Catholic Church had been uncomfortable with Mokhehle's strong association with Nkrumah and Sobukwe. Accordingly, it supported the formation of the Basutoland National Party (hereafter just the National Party) under three Catholics, Chief Leabua Jonathan, Patrik 'Mota and Gabriel Manyeli, in 1957. Before the formation of this splinter party, the Catholics had plans to form a Christian Democratic Party to counter the Congress Party, which it regarded as communist in ideology; by initiating and supporting the formation of the National Party, the Church sought to fight 'communism' in any guise it took in Lesotho (Machobane 1990: 285–87).

The National Party had several distinctive features. It was friendly towards the chiefs, and was prepared to work with the Apartheid government in South Africa – something that the Congress Party was strongly opposed to at the time. The Congress Party's approach left little room for women's political participation; the National Party capitalised on this and championed women's rights and political involvement. Lebua Jonathan, as a chief, had gained experience in the colonial administration and in the Regent Paramount Chieftainess 'Mantšebo's court. The National Party also had financial and other support from Europeans, Catholic missionaries and the colonial government – all influential and powerful actors that worked to direct the rural populations' voting patterns.

In October 1957, Chief S.S. Matete launched the Marema-Tlou Party. Matete had abandoned his position on the National Council in 1956, when he was still a member of the Congress Party. He believed that the political and economic crisis at the time was due to the incompetence of the Regent Paramount Chieftainess 'Mantšebo, who surrounded herself with weak advisors. He advocated for her removal and the installation of the rightful heir, Bereng Seeiso. Along with some chiefs and their supporters who were apprehensive of the commoners taking over the country's government, he broke away from the Congress Party. Khaketla, the editor of the Congress Party's newspaper (*The Warrior*) also broke away and formed the Basutoland Freedom Party (BFP), and the two merged in 1962, to form the Marematlou Freedom Party. While Mokhehle was never committed to the installation of Bereng Seeiso or the internal affairs of chieftainship in general, and wanted to see the monarchy stripped of its powers, the Freedom Party pushed for the executive powers of the monarchy to be made constitutional (Nyeko 2002b: 164–65).

Despite the Catholics' accusations that Mokhehle and his party were communists, there was also a Communist Party of Lesotho, though it remained small and less significant. With an estimated membership of about six hundred people, its impact remained minimal. It was launched by John Motloheloa in November 1961. Motloheloa was an ex-member of the Communist Party of South Africa, and a South African refugee following the Suppression of Communism Act of 1950. The Communist Party of Lesotho openly sold literature such as the *World Marxist Review* on the streets of Maseru. It advanced that it would 'act as an independent party of the workers and peasants of Lesotho, aiming at a Socialist Republic of Lesotho' (Halpern, cited in Nyeko 2002b: 167).

In 1961, the National Council passed a resolution calling for self-governance. The King, Moshoeshoe II, appointed a new Constitutional Commission to pave the way for independence. The Commission completed its mandate in 1963. Thereafter, the representatives of the National Council – along with Duncan Sandys, Secretary of State for the Colonies – held formal negotiations in London from April to May 1964 to determine the transition from colonial rule to self-government. These meetings established tentative dates for independence elections and made a resolution to select a parliamentary form of government for the Basotho. The colonial administration would govern jointly for a year to ensure a smooth transition. In 1965, Lesotho finally held elections; over 56 per cent of the adult population above the age of 21 voted. The National Party won most of the rural constituencies, guaranteeing its victory. On 4 October 1966, Lesotho officially attained its national independence from Britain (Aerni-Flessner 2018: 49–56).

Summary

This chapter has focused on the economic side of the liberation struggle in Lesotho. With restricted movement across borders, increasing poverty and reduced economic opportunities, the Basotho became more aggressive in their political pursuit of reforming commerce. With differing ideological positions and levels of efficiency, they pressured the colonial administration to open local commerce to Basotho. Their activities harboured a political consciousness that stoked the independence movements. As a result, commerce became the battleground for the liberation struggle. Basotho drew on new experiences in South Africa and missionary education to defend their society and call for economic justice, and fought to have a meaningful say and level of participation in the economic matters of their country.

The Progressive Association articulated urban challenges, while the League of Commoners, and later the Congress Party, radicalised the movement towards self-rule and economic determination. The Congress Party incorporated the rural masses into the struggle, but with a shift away from a regional outlook to a struggle along nationalistic lines. Africans in the wider region now focused on liberating the emergent states within colonially defined borders.

The Congress Party promised to fight for the return of the conquered lands. Though justifiable under their circumstances, this legitimised the colonial borders. The result was twofold: on the one hand, rigid constructions of national identities, belonging and territoriality were confirmed, and on the other, the vision to liberate the region as a whole fragmented. Lesotho attained its independence before South Africa. In the last part of this book, we consider the repercussions of this fragmented solidarity.

NOTES

1. Usually, these would be selected ordinary people with close relations to the chieftainship through marriage, or progressive farmers, civil servants and mine workers who were able to accumulate some assets and livestock over time. In Chapter 5 of *The Anti-Politics Machine* ('The Bovine Mystique: A Study of Power, Property, Livestock in Rural Lesotho'), Ferguson (1994) shows that young men went to the mines to build their flock and head of cattle for a variety of purposes, including procuring bridewealth (*lobola, Mahali*), accumulation, insurance or retirement plans. Cattle also acted as a 'place-holder' for a man in the community in his absence. Some people made their fortunes differently: in some cases, if a chief had a sexual relationship with someone's wife, a common courtesy was for the chief to reward the husband with land or livestock in order to appease the man. Though this is not widely documented, it was a common practice and persists in different forms.
2. *LNA, Basutoland Progressive Association, S3/22/2/1*, Constitution of Basutoland Progressive Association.
3. *LNA, Trade, S3/26/1/10*, Proceedings of the Licensing Board Meeting, Qacha's Nek, 13 June 1927.
4. Ibid.
5. *LNA, Trade, S3/26/1/10*, Appeal of a rejected licence from one Indian trader to the Assistant Commissioner, Qacha's Nek, 17 June 1927.
6. *LNA, Basutoland Progressive Association, S3/22/2/1*, BPA to the Assistant Commissioner, Teyateyaneng, 13 November 1935.
7. Interview with Ashley Thorn, European business owner in Lesotho, Roma, October 16, 2013.
8. *LNA, Lekhotla la Bafo, S3/22/1/1*, LLB to the High Commissioner, Cape Town, 22 October 1927.
9. Ibid.
10. Ibid.
11. Ibid.
12. *LNA, Lekhotla la Bafo, S3/22/1/1*, Report of the meeting of LLB in Maseru, 11 August 1929.
13. *NULA, Trade, LC 23/11*, District Commissioner in Leribe to the Licensing Board, 27 August 1957.
14. Ibid.

REFERENCES

Aerni-Flessner, J. 2018. *Dreams for Lesotho: Independence, Foreign Assistance, and Development*. Notre Dame, Indiana: University of Notre Dame Press.

Ashton, H. 1967. *The Basuto: A Social Study of Traditional and Modern Lesotho*. London: Oxford University Press.

Edgar, R. 1987. *Prophets with Honour: A Documentary History of Lekhotla la Bafo*. Johannesburg: Ravan Press.

Ferguson, J. 1994. *The Anti-Politics Machine: 'Development', Depoliticisation, and Bureaucratic Power in Lesotho*. London: University of Minnesota Press.

Gill, S. 1993. *A Short History of Lesotho: From the Late Stone Age until the 1993 Election*. Roma: National University of Lesotho, Institute of Southern African Studies.

Leys, R. 1981. 'Some Observations on Class Differentiation and Class Conflict within the Labour Reserve of Basutoland: Collected Seminar Papers by the Institute of Commonwealth Studies'. Retrieved 16 June 2015 from http://sas-space.sas.ac.uk/4099/1/Roger_Leys_-_Some_observations_on_class_differentiation_and_class_conflict_within_the_labour_reserve_of_basutoland.pdf.

Machobane, L.B.B.J. 1990. *Government and Change in Lesotho, 1800–1966: A Study of Political Institutions*. London: Macmillan Press.

Matlosa, K., and C. Sello. 2005. *Political Parties and Democracy in Lesotho*. Johannesburg: Electoral Institute for Sustainable Democracy in Africa.

Murray, C. 1981. *Families Divided: The Impact of Migrant Labour in Lesotho*. Cambridge: Cambridge University Press.

Nyeko, B. 2002a. 'Resistance to Colonial Rule and the Emergence of Anti-Colonial Movements', in N.W. Pule and M. Thabane (eds), *Essays on Aspects of the Political Economy of Lesotho*. Roma: Department of History, National University of Lesotho, pp. 131–51.

———. 2002b. 'The Independence Movement, 1952–1966', in N.W. Pule and M. Thabane (eds), *Essays on Aspects of the Political Economy of Lesotho*. Roma: Department of History, National University of Lesotho, pp. 153–72.

Pim, A. 1935. *Financial and Economic Position of Basutoland: Report of the Commission Appointed by the Secretary of State for Dominion Affairs*. London: His Majesty's Stationery Office.

Weisfelder, R.F. 1974. 'Early Voices of Protest in Basutoland: The Progressive Association and Lekhotla La Bafo', *African Studies Review* 17(2): 397–409.

———. 1999. *Political Contention in Lesotho, 1952–1965*. Roma: Institute of Southern African Studies.

Part III

Lesotho's Postcolonial Counter-Revolution and Resistance to It

CHAPTER 6

The Developmental State and Lesotho's Counter-Revolution, 1966–1986

Introduction

As a former British Crown colony, Lesotho opted to follow capitalism after independence. Like other African countries, it attained independence after the Second World War within a plural global economic paradigm. Before that, the dominant global economic system had been built on self-regulating markets, the gold standard, the liberal state and the balance of power in the West (Polanyi 1944; Hann and Hart 2009).

After the war, the liberal economy expanded under the stewardship of the United States, while the post-war economic boom of the 1950s and 1960s was achieved through a Keynesian combination of world markets and political control of the economy by the leading industrial nations. Thereafter, the developmental state became the engine of economic growth. Other countries opted for a socialist economy under the leadership of the Soviet Union (Keynes 1936; Hann and Hart 2009).

We see in this chapter that the National Party government accordingly took a leading role in the development of the economy. It attempted to industrialise and modernise various sectors of the economy, including commerce, manufacturing, tourism, agriculture, finance and transport. Its main approach was to create government parastatals with responsibility for developing specific sectors, often with minimal foreign investment, as the developmental state model prescribed. Given its status as a reservoir of cheap labour, and the fact that the colonial government had not invested in its development, Lesotho was faced with many challenges. For one thing, it continued to depend on foreign aid, South Africa and the Southern African Customs Union (Ward 1967; Lundahl and Peterson 1991; Lundahl et al. 2003).

The government came to dominate Lesotho's development institutions, which were meant to industrialise the economy. It oppressed, excluded and neglected Basotho traders and undermined their economic solidarity. As in the colonial period, Basotho continued to depend on their associations and co-operatives to advance and protect their interests, with the aim of overthrowing European traders and attaining economic independence.

This chapter demonstrates that Basotho successes came from self-organisation, and investigates the ways in which the Basotho negotiated new partnerships with large South African companies. It also argues that neocolonialism undermined popular initiatives, while development was used as an altruistic mask for the advancement of despotism across various spheres of the economy, commerce included.

Developing Lesotho's Economy after National Independence: LNDC and BEDCO

In 1966, 75–90 per cent of Lesotho's imports came from South Africa. This increased by 32 per cent between 1965 and 1966, to R22 million. Compared to these imports, Lesotho's exports to South Africa in 1966 amounted only to some R4 million, a 7 per cent decline from its exports to South Africa in 1965. Lesotho's exports comprised livestock, grain, vegetables, wool and mohair, hides and skins, and diamonds. Wool and mohair constituted 64 per cent of exports to South Africa in 1966 (Ward 1967: 364–65). Of the three former British High Commission territories of Botswana, Lesotho and Swaziland, Lesotho had the lowest Gross Domestic Product (GDP) per capita in 1966, at only US$35. Botswana had the highest at $312, and Swaziland had about $192 (ibid.: 355–68).

Commerce, in terms of GDP contribution, came third after agriculture and government services, and continued to be dominated by European traders. In the 1974/75 financial year, agriculture contributed 32 per cent to GDP, increasing to 44 per cent by 1979/80. Commerce contributed 10 per cent, increasing to 14 per cent, in the same years.[1] The government observed that: 'Of this trade, by far the greater part is in the hands of a few expatriate firms ... expatriate businesses were on average substantially larger than local businesses'. It pointed out that European traders' 'share of the trade was far greater than these figures would suggest. Of the Basotho retailers recorded, over 80% had a monthly turnover of under R1,200', while 'the turnover of European-controlled retailers was estimated to range between R10,000 and R15,000 per month'. Above all, it noted that '[t]he disparities are even greater in the wholesale trade, which is virtually entirely in expatriate hands'.[2]

The National Party positioned itself as the ideal government to turn the economy around and create one that would be less dependent on external forces. Writing about the South African developmental state in the twentieth century, Freund highlights some of its managerial tenets, which were also visible in Lesotho: 'A key defining element is *agency*, the existence of a state-formed body that transcends bureaucratic rules; in Weberian terms, this means bureaucratic rule *plus* charisma' (Freund 2018: 6). South Africa played a similar role in Lesotho since it needed the latter's water (see Chapter 7).

From 1966 to 1970, Lesotho collaborated with the South African apartheid government, which played a significant role in Lesotho's development programmes. In particular, South Africa played a major role in the establishment and funding of the Lesotho National Development Corporation (LNDC). Established in 1967, the LNDC was to facilitate domestic investment, industrialisation and economic diversification beyond small-scale rural agriculture. It was mandated to attract and cultivate a favourable business environment for foreign investment and assist the government in designing industrialisation policies .[3]

In line with its developmental outlook, the government charismatically maintained that it would 'not hesitate to take a leading investment role, usually through [the] LNDC'.[4] Its long-term industrialisation policy was geared towards developing the non-agricultural sectors of the economy. It noted that: 'The limited agricultural resources of the country cannot provide gainful employment opportunities'. Therefore, in the long term:

> non-agricultural productive activities ... will become a major path for economic development. The development of non-agricultural activities is, therefore, an integral part of the long-term development perspective ... The establishment in 1967 of the Lesotho National Development Corporation ... is a decisive step in this direction.[5]

From then on, the LNDC attracted investors to establish hotels, lodges and shopping centres in the urban areas of the country.[6] Its major activities included the establishment of the Lesotho Electricity Corporation, the Lesotho Airways Corporation, the Produce Marketing Corporation, the Livestock Marketing Corporation, the Lesotho Bank, Lesotho National Bus Services and the Lesotho Tourist Corporation.[7]

The LNDC was funded by South Africa and managed by South African personnel from its inception until the early 1970s. The government employed expatriates rather than local educated people, since the majority of the latter were members of the Congress Party. Ajulu (1995: 10) correctly argues that:

> the Lesotho National Development Corporation was not only set up with the assistance of Afrikaner capital … its senior personnel were recruited from the Anglo-American and Rembrandt conglomerates in South Africa. [Its purpose was] to largely exclude the educated and commercial classes of the BCP from the bureaucracy as well as from the parastatals. [As a result], this led to the domination of the economy by South African commercial capital and the exclusion of indigenous classes of property from the 'fruits of independence'.

Conceived as it was in right-wing capitalist ideology and Catholic conservatism, the National Party had aligned with the South African government to gain support against the Congress Party (Ajulu 1995: 11). Despite financial support from the South African government, however, the National Party could not expand its political support base, and it lost the 1970 election to the Congress Party. Thereafter, the country was subjected to an overt dictatorship.

As the results of the elections were being announced in January 1970, with the Congress Party leading, the state-run Radio Lesotho stopped broadcasting. It announced that the Prime Minister would be addressing the nation later that day. When the time came for Leabua Jonathan's speech, he announced that there had been widespread intimidation during the elections. This was contrary to observers' reports that the elections had been free and fair. Jonathan declared a State of Emergency and suspended the constitution in order to ensure law and order. Constitutional rule collapsed, and members of opposition parties across the country were violently harassed, and some imprisoned. As members of the major opposition party, Congress Party members were selected for brutal torture (Khaketla 1971: 208).

South Africa lost faith in the National Party government and reduced its financial support to Lesotho as a result. Lesotho was forced to seek other avenues of financial assistance. It turned to the international arena by adopting various of the United Nations' protocols. This forced the government to lessen its collaboration with South Africa; it now criticised apartheid openly and accepted African National Congress refugees (Ajulu 1995: 12–13; Pule 2002b: 180–84).

Once South Africa pulled its resources out, Lesotho's government opened the economy to foreign investment and international aid. Through the LNDC, it attracted foreign investors to establish industries producing pottery, umbrellas, sheepskin products, candles, electric lamps, furniture and hand-loomed rugs.[8] By 1978, the LNDC had attracted private investment of approximately R2.5 million.[9] It had also assisted in the formation of thirty-six local manufacturing enterprises. Nine of these firms were involved in agriculture-related products such as canning, milling, distilling and weaving. Sixteen manufactured building materials, while the rest processed products from imported material.

In March 1975, the government created the Basotho Enterprises Development Corporation (BEDCO) as a subsidiary of the LNDC, with financial and technical assistance from the Canadian International Development Agency (Ngwenya 1977: 23). BEDCO's major task was to develop Basotho-owned businesses through training, provision of technical services and small-scale credit.[10] Explaining its creation, the government stated: 'Businesses run by the Basotho people themselves were rare in the years before independence'. As a result, to 'help build up an entrepreneurial class, to develop skills and to provide employment, BEDCO was formed in 1975 with a broadly-based mandate of providing assistance to the small business'.[11]

BEDCO's programmes were parachuted into the economy by dictatorial fiat. Their prescriptions were expected to automatically develop the economy, while many Basotho traders were denied access to business loans. For example, in a government study two years after BEDCO's establishment, Ngwenya (1977: 30) discovered that: 'As of January 1977, loans amounting to R21,000 had been made to BEDCO subsidiaries with another R15,900 being given to nine separate enterprises. Few loans were disbursed [to ordinary Basotho]'. Basotho were marginalised and had to depend on their own initiatives.

The National Party government used its developmental role to justify its dictatorial actions. Both Ferguson (1994) and Aerni-Flessner (2018) argue that the National Party used development tools and knowledge to expand state power over impoverished rural communities through various agricultural and 'food-for-work' (*fato fato*) programmes. Because the National Party government's popular support was 'relatively weak, the development projects that it brought to the country contributed to a sense that progress was being made towards a desired vision for independence' (Aerni-Flessner 2018: 182).

Ferguson observes that development in Lesotho expanded the power of the state. He suggests that while the government promised to help a suffering and oppressed people, 'the hegemonic problematic of "development" is the principle means through which the question of poverty is depoliticized':

> The 'instrumental-effect' then, is two-fold: alongside the institutional effect of expanding bureaucratic state power is the conceptual or ideological effect of depoliticizing both poverty and the state … If the 'instrumental-effect' of a 'development' project end up [*sic*] forming any kind of strategically coherent or intelligible whole, this is it: the anti-politics machine. (1994: 256)

The Association of Traders in Lesotho

In its development pursuits, the government marginalised Basotho traders, the majority of whom were members of the opposition Congress Party.[12] As the country approached independence, the Basotho Traders' Association had become moribund. It was taken over by a group of influential Maseru-based Basotho traders, who were optimistic about the trade opportunities that would come with national independence. In 1965, plans to resuscitate the association began when Buta Phalatsi approached the Congress Party to assist traders in drafting a constitution, which would correlate with the party's co-operatives policy. The outcome was the formation of a team consisting of Buta Phalatsi, Ntsukunyane Mphanya and Thebe Tlale, who drafted the constitution.[13] Mphanya was at the time the Deputy General Secretary of the party and a trader who staunchly advocated co-operatives.[14]

In 1968, the Commission proposed changing the association's name to the 'Lesotho Chamber of Commerce'. This expressed Basotho traders' wish to control local trade after national independence, as a sign of victory over the Europeans-only Basutoland Chamber of Commerce.[15] The Registrar of Societies at the Lesotho Law Office rejected the name, informing Basotho traders in his letter of January 1968 that 'I could not register your Society under the name Lesotho Chamber of Commerce as this name had already been reserved by the Chamber of Commerce of Lesotho'.[16] As a result, when the association was registered in May, under the Societies Act of 1966, it was registered with a Sesotho name: 'Mokhatlo oa Bahoebi Lesotho' (literally, 'the Association of Traders in Lesotho', but popularly called the Basotho Traders Association, even in official communications). The association took off on a very high note, and it grew and spread across the whole country.[17]

It was governed by an Executive Committee, to be elected annually in the General Conference. The first Executive Committee of the association was composed of Buta Phalatsi (President), Maqhoaelane Hlekane (Vice-President) and Thabiso Santho (Chairman). Khatlako J. Rakhoabe was Vice-Chairman, Pitso Mafantiri the Secretary and Mohlouoa Ramakatane the Assistant Secretary. The only woman, 'Mankone Ramarou, was the Treasurer, while Sidwell Thakalekoala and Kholeli Sekhibane were Committee Members.[18]

The Traders Association had branches in all the districts of Lesotho. District branches had committees which were elected every September in a general meeting, and which consisted of a Chairman, Vice-Chairman, Secretary, Organising Secretary, Treasurer and two Committee Members. According to the association's constitution, membership was 'open to all traders trading in Lesotho, irrespective of race, colour or creed'.[19]

Upon admission, a member had to pay a registration fee of R2, and thereafter paid an annual subscription of the same amount. The association sought to encourage and promote stable and viable commercial and industrial activity. To achieve this, it first had to create an atmosphere conducive to business, in which Basotho traders could trade in fair competition with the foreign traders' monopoly. Its constitution stipulated that its primary objective was:

> To strive for the creation and maintenance of conditions to the maximum development of commercial and industrial activity in Lesotho and for the protection of Lesotho traders against monopoly enterprises, unfair competition from foreign business concerns and other similar practices inimical to the interests of Lesotho traders.[20]

The association launched several initiatives in an attempt to develop local trade for Basotho traders. It embarked on a massive membership recruitment campaign and disseminated the association's mission widely, and even hosted beauty pageants and trade fairs to raise funds and awareness (*Lesotho News*, vol. xxxvii, No. 2193, 8 July 1969: 1).[21] It held training workshops, seminars and public lectures for Basotho traders around the country to train them in business skills. Its mission was to help the Basotho traders to acquire the 'best skills in fields of commerce' and develop 'proficiency in business techniques', as well as to assist them to 'adopt advanced business methods' (*Lesotho News*, vol. xxxvi, No. 2149, 23 July 1968: 3).[22]

In some instances, the association worked with the government and selected international development institutions to advance Basotho traders' interests, although as I show later, this was short-lived. In partnership with the International Labour Organization (ILO) and the Ministry of Finance, Commerce and Industry, it launched the UN-sponsored 'Business Extension Services' in 1968. The ILO sent a UN Business Extension Advisor to facilitate the programme (*Lesotho Times*, Vol. VI, No. 169, 26 April 1968: 6; *Lesotho News*, vol. xxxvi, no. 2149, 23 July 1968: 3; *Lesotho News*, vol. xxxvii, no. 2177, 4 March 1969: 1). He travelled around the country with Mafantiri, Phalatsi and government officials, training members of the association and other Basotho traders through courses such as 'Bookkeeping', 'Statistical Records', 'The Employment Act', 'Income Tax Law and its Implications', and 'Buying and Selling Policies' (*Lesotho News*, vol. xxxvi, no. 2149, 23 July 1968: 3; *Lesotho News*, vol. xxxvii, no. 2177, 4 March 1969: 1; *Lesotho News*, vol. xxxvii, No. 2208, 28 October 1969: 1).[23]

Basotho Traders' Bulk-Buying Syndicate ('Thekommoho')

In 1969, the Traders Association established a bulk-buying co-operative as its economic wing. It was registered under the Co-operative Societies Act of 1966 under the name 'Basotho Traders' Bulk Buying Syndicate', although it was popularly called 'Thekommoho', which means 'buying together' (*Lesotho News*, 14 October 1969: 1). The co-operative started with about four hundred members, of whom 220 were shareholders (*Lesotho News*, 2 October 1970: 3). Basotho traders had hoped to establish branches in all the districts of Lesotho, as well as a bank. When the co-operative collapsed in 1970, only two branches had been established, in the Maseru and Leribe districts. I will return to this later.

Buta Phalatsi was elected Chairman, and his Deputy was Ambrose Makhobalo; the Organising Secretary was Maqhoaelane Hlekane and L.L. Shuping was the Treasurer. Members of the Committee were R. Masupha, Teboho Possa, J.R. Taunyane and M. Maime (*Lesotho News*, 1 July 1969: 2). Pitso Mafantiri was appointed as a representative of South African wholesalers and manufacturers in Lesotho because of his business expertise and experience as a bookkeeper. Since Lesotho was now independent, Basotho traders felt that they could no longer buy stock from South African suppliers through European agencies, such as Whitakers.[24]

Through the co-operative, Basotho traders bought stock from South African manufacturers and wholesalers on credit. A consignment was payable within a period of thirty days (*Lesotho News*, 14 October 1969: 1). The foundation that the Basotho traders laid ensured that their co-operative took off successfully. In Maseru, the branch started with capital amounting to some R2,000. Its financial statements showed that in June 1970, its purchases amounted to R192,000 (*Lesotho News*, 2 October 1970: 3). In Leribe, Ramafokisi Mofokeng pointed out that their branch started with little capital, but was able to deposit around R50,000 in the bank daily. Soon the business became more lucrative, and the co-operative could deposit about R100,000 in the bank daily to repay its suppliers in

South Africa.[25] G.G. Malahleha poetically described this, saying, 'it actually took off like a house on fire'.[26]

Several factors were responsible for the co-operative's success. Firstly, Thekommoho sold stock to Basotho traders at low wholesale prices.[27] Secondly, traders had formerly paid a Maize Levy to the South African government when they imported maize and maize products into Lesotho. All traders in Lesotho had to increase their prices on these staple foods as a result. The South African government used the revenue collected from the Maize Levy to compensate farmers in South Africa at times of crop failure caused by natural disasters. By the end of 1969, the South African government had instructed its farmers to take insurance instead, and the Maize Levy was removed.[28] The co-operative took advantage of this and dropped their prices on these products, while European traders did not.

Lastly, Thekommoho's affiliation with South African firms revolutionised advertising in Lesotho. The suppliers issued the co-operative brochures, advertising various promotions. The co-operative gave these brochures to Basotho traders, who then distributed them to customers. According to Joe Motsoahae, a local trader and member of Thekommoho, this was a new phenomenon in Lesotho's local business. It created such a colossal spectacle that it captured customers' attention and attracted more of them.[29] Prior to this, advertising was done in newspapers and only the well-off could afford it – these, it goes without saying, being predominantly European traders (Mokuku 2000: 51–62).

The Defeat of Basotho Traders

The government and the European traders, however, saw the growth and popularity of Thekommoho as a threat. For the government, it was a political threat, in that many members and leaders of the Basotho Traders' Association and the co-operative were also followers and even active members of the Congress Party. The co-operative was formed a few months before Lesotho's general elections in January 1970. Undoubtedly, the organisation boosted the Congress Party's campaigns. Not surprisingly, the government accused Basotho business owners of using their businesses for political purposes, and the Prime Minister, Leabua Jonathan, threatened that 'businessmen who allowed their business premises to be used as political platforms [will] have their trading licences suspended' (*Lesotho News*, 14 October 1969: 1).

European traders saw Basotho traders as an economic challenge, because the latter were likely to take business away from them through the co-operative. Initially, European traders responded by approaching Thekommoho leaders and requesting that they reconsider their prices, but the Basotho refused. Joe Motsoahae pointed out that in Maseru the impact was felt by European traders, especially Frasers. He recalled that

> we became so powerful in such a short space of time that it made people like Frasers to cry … [Before the establishment of Thekommoho] we used to flock at Frasers, pushing each other, going in the morning. Frasers was busy right through to four o'clock; [but when Thekommoho took off] it was so quiet [in Frasers] that you could hear a mosquito fly'.[30]

The National Party government and European traders collaborated to undermine the co-operative. During the State of Emergency, they attacked Basotho traders and the leadership of the co-operative and the Traders Association. The government raided and burnt businesses of some prominent leaders and members (Mphanya 2010: 85–89). Remembering this time, Malahleha lamented: 'My own brother was beaten there at 'Maseribane's [place] for two nights in succession, non-stop! From 22:00 to 04:00 in the morning. You get it? That was terrible because he was a businessman in Mafeteng and he naturally … did support the Congress'.[31]

Selected members of the Traders Association and leaders of the co-operative were imprisoned, together with various opposition members, and the co-operative was shut down. Basotho traders' stocks were raided by the Police Mobile Unit (*The Lesotho Monitor*, 6–13 June 2008: 10). The government alleged that it had uncovered a Congress Party plot to spread violence across the country. The police claimed that they had found twenty-one inflammable bombs, a 303 rifle and ammunition, swords, axes and knives in the shops of some leaders of the Traders' Association and other Basotho traders (*Lesotho News*, 14 April 1970: 1; Poulter 1979: 92).

After the State of Emergency, those of its members who had not been imprisoned resuscitated the co-operative, relocating from Thabiso Santho's premises to Buta Phalatsi's store. Just when Thekommoho was starting to take shape again, the government sued it for not paying the Maize Levy. The co-operative operated from October 1969 to June 1970. As previously discussed, towards the end of 1969 the South African government removed the Maize Levy, which made it possible for the co-operative to reduce its prices on imported maize and maize products. European traders approached the Lesotho government to introduce a tax on these items, and Chief Leabua Jonathan's regime agreed, because it was in financial crisis after the State of Emergency.[32]

Thekommoho did not comply with the tax and the government sued it. The High Court found it guilty and instructed it to pay the government about R90,000, an amount which it could not pay at that time. As a result, the co-operative's stocks and property were auctioned by the High Court to repay the tax. Joe Motsoahae recalled with sorrow that after the court case, 'Thekommoho was closed … Everything was sold. The High Court sold them … My heart was so painful'.[33]

Thereafter, the National Party government maintained a tight grip on the economy and ruled by decree. First, it promulgated the Trade Ordinance of 1973, designed to expand the powers of the Minister of Commerce in business licencing matters by giving him the authority to 'amend or make additions to the [law, arbitrarily,] by notice to be published in the Gazette'.[34]

Furthermore, the new law gave the Minister control over the appointment of the Appeal Board of Licences.[35] The Minister was given the authority to prescribe documents to be used and fees to be paid, to decide conditions under which licences were to be issued and to set hours and days of business. He could even 'prescribe standards of morality … to be served by holders of trading licenses'.[36]

In contrast to the government's general support for European traders, however, the Minister of Commerce and Industry at this time, Joel Moitse, favoured Basotho in business, and encouraged the Basotho to take control of the local economy. Before his appointment, Moitse had been Pro-Vice-Chancellor of the National University of Lesotho and a poultry businessman (*Lehlaahlela*, December 1975: 3). In January 1975, he held a training workshop for over a hundred Basotho traders in the district of Mafeteng. At the end of the workshop, he delivered a controversial closing speech, informing traders that it was the government's policy to make sure that business in Lesotho was finally put into the hands of Basotho, while foreigners should only operate big firms in the country. He polemically concluded: 'Our enemies are scared of what we stand for and who we are' (*Lehlaahlela*, January 1975: 4). The *Lehlaahlela* (ibid.), a local newspaper, described the mood of the workshop's participants and the Minister as revolutionary. On another occasion, the Minister added: 'Political independence was useless if the country could not be economically independent' (*Mochochonono*, 20 June 1975: 6).

The Prime Minister unceremoniously removed Moitse from his position in June 1975, without even informing him why he was being sacked (*Mochochonono*, 19 June 1975: 1; *Lehlaahlela*, December 1975: 3). Commenting on his dismissal, the *Lehlaahlela* newspaper (ibid.) suggested that he had been sacked because of his pan-Africanist views, adding that 'we should not forget how much he was devoted to making sure that business in Lesotho was finally put into the hands of Basotho'.

Moitse's sacking left the Basotho defenceless, and the government moved to consolidate its power over local commerce. One outstanding Basotho entrepreneurial effort that it sabotaged was the 'Makro deal'. Two groups of Basotho traders successfully opened wholesale businesses: 'Metla-khola Cash & Carry (chaired by M.T. Ramakatane), in the Maseru District, and Bana-ba-Khoale Cash & Carry (chaired by S.B. Monyake) in the Mafeteng District. To expand their business, the two successfully negotiated with Makro Cash & Carry, a South Africa-based wholesaler, such that the latter would open a branch in Lesotho. The agreement was that Basotho traders would be the major shareholders (*Mochochonono*, 27 February 1975: 7; *Lehlaahlela*, November 1975: 2).

To counter the Makro deal and keep the Basotho down, the government negotiated with Metro Cash & Carry, another South Africa-based wholesaler, in order for it to establish a branch in Maseru instead (*Mochochonono*, 6 November 1975: 4). The government gave Metro a building already promised to Makro and the Basotho traders, and the Makro deal failed (*Lehlaahlela*, November 1975: 2). By the mid-1970s, the government had tightened its grip on the local economy with virtually no opposition from Basotho traders.

The Lesotho Chamber of Commerce and Industry

To consolidate its mission, the government partnered with European traders to form an umbrella business association in 1976. Their aim was to establish a body representing all communities in Lesotho – Europeans, Indians and Basotho. At the end of 1975, the Chamber of Commerce met with the Prime Minister and Senior Cabinet Secretaries to negotiate.[37] In January 1976, the newly appointed Minister of Commerce and Industry, K.T.J. Rakhetla, called a public meeting to address the business community – the Basotho Traders' Association and Lesotho Chamber of Commerce.[38]

Politically weakened and economically marginal, the Basotho traders responded positively to this call and participated in the formation of the new organisation. Two years earlier, the government had violently suppressed the Congress Party's attempt to overthrow it. The Congress Party held that the National Party was not a legitimate government, as it had seized power unlawfully in 1970. As a result, in 1974, the Congress Party planned and launched a series of violent attacks against the government, targeting police stations with the aim of acquiring arms and ammunition to topple the government. The military brutally suppressed this revolt, and many leaders and members of the Congress Party fled into exile, while others were imprisoned (Pule 2002b: 180–84). Ajulu (1995: 11) observes: 'Non-exiled factions of the Congress Party, who were in business ... defected to [the National Party government] to take advantage of access to the state for purposes of continued capital accumulation'.

Thus, in a speech delivered when the new body was launched, J.C. Masithela, President of the Basotho Traders' Association, supported its formation.[39] He acknowledged that the meeting came about because of a proposal made by the Minister of Commerce and Industry, Rakhetla, who maintained that it was high time that the two associations 'put aside petty differences which [had] existed over the years, and form[ed] a united front for the benefit of ... traders and of the commerce and industry in Lesotho'. Masithela confirmed this point: 'It is true that some form of misunderstanding did exist between the two organizations'. He promised that 'at the conclusion of our deliberations, such differences will start to melt away and be regarded as a thing of the past'.

On 3 February 1976, Basotho and Europeans met to begin talks on how to launch the new organisation.[40] The same day, they elected a transitional committee of eleven members tasked to establish the organisation. The committee drafted the constitution and held consultative meetings with the business community around the country.[41] Coming from around the country, the following business owners were elected to the Steering Committee: I.H. Dare, R. Matji, L. Makoa, S. Molapo, N.E. Cretchley, J.M. Nthongoa, H.T. Mitchell, M. Khoase, S.M. Yeats, S. Possa and A. Newman. Dare was unanimously elected to be the chair of the Committee.

In March 1976, representatives of the business community held another meeting to discuss their findings,[42] and in May 1976, they held their final meeting and launched their association,[43] adopting the name 'the Lesotho Chamber of Commerce and Industry' (LCCI). A constitution was also adopted, providing for the creation of the LCCI as an umbrella organisation which represented district associations, not individuals. Individual members were required to pay an annual subscription fee calculated at a rate of 5 per cent of their total licence fees. Membership was voluntary.

The Chamber launched its operations with a strong recruitment campaign. By the end of 1976, it had 625 members across the country,[44] and a year later, its membership had doubled to around 1,200.[45] By the 1980s, the Chamber had attracted several big businesses and corporations in Lesotho, which joined as Associate Members (Montši and Associates 1992: 5).[46]

From the late 1970s, the Chamber shifted its orientation towards Basotho business owners, beginning with the election of M.J. Nthongoa as the first Mosotho President and R. Matji as General Secretary. These two figures adopted an Afrocentric policy, which began with aggressive recruitment of Basotho business owners (Montši and Associates 1992: 1). The new leadership expanded the scope of the Chamber beyond Lesotho, proactively embracing relations with African and pan-Africanist chambers of commerce at regional, continental and international levels. It formed relations with the National African Chamber of Commerce and Industry (NAFCOC) – the South African black business chamber – as well as the Zimbabwean National Chamber of Commerce (ZNCC) and the International Chamber of Commerce (ICC), and it was a founding member of the African Chamber of Commerce (*Lesotho Business Magazine*, February/March 1982: 25; March/April 1983: 12; March/April 1984: 11; February/March 1985: 13–15; March/April 1985: 5).

Given its pan-African orientation, the Chamber increasingly became an organisation of small Basotho traders, and was less attractive to many big businesses, which began to distance themselves from it (Montši and Associates 1992: 1). In 1992, the government commissioned Montši and Associates, a Cape Town consultancy company, to review the Chamber's ability to meet its mandates and members' expectations. Amongst other findings, the report revealed that: 'In its first few years the Chamber was quite integrated, and it strived to represent the entire business community of Lesotho'. Over time, as it followed a robust recruitment campaign, 'Basotho traders became a force in the Chamber and the movement began to shift in its outlook and emphasis in favour of Basotho traders and their problems' (ibid.). As a result, European traders started withdrawing their participation in the new organisation. After independence, many left the country and their hegemony dwindled significantly.

Summary

National independence further legitimised Lesotho's territorial definition. With this, a discourse of dependency on externality emerged. This was a shift away from a practical understanding that Lesotho was always connected to the regional economy, and in particular to South Africa. Development discourse and practice were accordingly built on the hope to reverse this order by creating an 'independent national economy' that was less reliant on external forces. The new government, however, played its developmental role in a dictatorial manner. It undermined Basotho economic initiatives in order to preserve its position in power and its alliance with Europeans, and it used development programmes and institutions (the LNDC, BEDCO and LCCI) to expand despotism. Effectively, the National Party consolidated the foundations for neocolonialism in postcolonial Lesotho.

The temporary rise of Basotho economic fortunes and solidarity is attributable to the Basotho's ability to self-organise internally. Also important (and novel) was the way in which they attempted to practically dismantle national constrictions between Lesotho and South Africa. Despite the reality of oppressive apartheid in South Africa, they successfully negotiated with South African firms to solve the persistent problems of credit and supply of stock that put them behind European and Indian traders. The violence of the National Party government, however, did not only kill Basotho entrepreneurial flair but also a realisation that Lesotho could negotiate favourable terms with South Africa despite inherent hierarchies. In many ways, Thekommoho is a classic case to demonstrate this reality in the economic history of modern Lesotho.

NOTES

1. *NULA, Lesotho Second Five-Year Development Plan, 1975/76–1979/80, Volume I*, 24.
2. *NULA, Lesotho First Five-Year Development Plan, 1970/1–1974/5*, 122.
3. *NULA, Lesotho National Development Corporation Annual Report, 2000/01*, 2.
4. *NULA, Lesotho Second Five-Year Development Plan, 1975/76–1979/80, Volume I*, 64.
5. *NULA, Lesotho First Five-Year Development Plan, 1970/1–1974/5*, 25.
6. *NULA, Lesotho Third Five-Year Development Plan, 1980–1985*, 217.
7. *NULA, Lesotho Second Five-Year Development Plan, 1975/76–1979/80, Volume II*, 4–5.
8. Ibid., 13.
9. *NULA, Lesotho Third Five-Year Development Plan, 1980–1985*, 218.
10. *NULA, Basotho Enterprises Development Corporation 10 Years Anniversary Special Issue*, n.d., 3–14; *NULA, Lesotho Third Five Year Development Plan*, 1980–1985, 219.
11. *NULA, Lesotho Review of Commerce and Industry, 1982/3*. In 1980, the government passed Act No. 9 to make BEDCO independent from the LNDC.
12. Part of the material in this section and in the two subsequent ones was originally published in an article submitted to *African Economic History*, 45(1):110–137, © 2017 the Board of Regents of the University of Wisconsin. Republished courtesy of the University of Wisconsin Press.
13. Ntsukunyane Mphanya was elected onto the Executive Committee of the BCP in 1963.
14. Interview with Ntsukunyane Mphanya, Mosotho politician and businessman, Mapoteng, August 2009.
15. Interview with Mphanya, August 2009.
16. *Lesotho Legal Office* (Hereafter LLO) *Legal Document No. 68/4*, Registrar General to MBL, Maseru, 22 January 1968.
17. Interview with Pitso Mafantiri, Founding Member of Thekommoho and Representative of South African Companies, Borokhoaneng, July 2009.
18. *LLO, Legal Document No. 68/4*, MBL to Registrar General, Maseru, 19 June 1968.
19. *LLO, Legal Document No. 68/4*, Constitution of MBL, Maseru, 31 May 1968.

20. Ibid.
21. Interview with Mafantiri, July 2009.
22. *LLO, Legal Document No. 68/4*, Constitution of MBL, Maseru, 31 May 1968.
23. Interview with Mafantiri, July 2009; *LNA, Local Trading and General*, TRD/1 Vol. IV, MBL to the Commissioner of Commerce and Industries, Maseru, 10 September 1968.
24. Interview with Mafantiri, July 2009.
25. Interview with Mofokeng, September 2009.
26. Interview with G.G. Malahleha, retired teacher, businessman and former Secretary of Thekommoho, Maseru, August 2009.
27. Interview with Mafantiri, July 2009; interview with Ramafokisi Mofokeng, former businessman and founding member of the Leribe branch of Thekommoho, Leribe, September 2009.
28. Interview with Joe Motsoahae, retired businessman and former member of Thekommoho, Bloemfontein, August 2010.
29. Interview with Motsoahae, August 2010.
30. Ibid.
31. Interview with Malahleha, August 2009.
32. Interview with Motsoahae, August 2010.
33. Ibid.
34. *NULA*, Section 20, *Order No. 20 of 1973*, 34.
35. *NULA*, Section 21 (1), *Order No. 20 of 1973*, 34.
36. *NULA*, Section 21 (1), Articles A to K, *Order No. 20 of 1973*, 34.
37. *Lesotho Chamber of Commerce and Industry* (hereafter LCCI), Address by K.B.T. Jandrell, Chairman of the Lesotho Chamber of Commerce to the Meeting of Representatives of Commerce and Industry in Lesotho, Holiday Inn, Maseru, 5 May 1976.
38. *LCCI*, Minutes of the Opening Address by I.H. Dare, Vice-Chairman of the Lesotho Chamber of Commerce in the Meeting of Representatives of Commerce and Industry in Lesotho, Holiday Inn, Maseru, 3 February 1976.
39. *LCCI*, Minutes of the Address by J.C. Masithela, President of the Basotho Traders' Association to a Meeting of Representatives of Commerce and Industry in Lesotho, Holiday Inn, Maseru, 5 May 1976.
40. *LCCI*, Minutes of the Opening Address by I.H. Dare, Vice-Chairman of the Lesotho Chamber of Commerce in a Meeting of Representatives of Commerce and Industry in Lesotho, Holiday Inn, Maseru, 3 February 1976.
41. *LCCI*, Minutes of the Meeting of Representatives of the Trading Community in Lesotho, Holiday Inn, Maseru, 3 February 1976.
42. *LCCI*, Minutes of the Meeting of the Steering Committee, Maseru Library, Maseru, 18 March 1976.
43. *LCCI*, Minutes of the Second Control Meeting of Representatives of Commerce and Industry in Lesotho, Holiday Inn, Maseru, 5 May 1976.
44. *LCCI*, Minutes of the Executive Committee of the Lesotho Chamber of Commerce and Industry, Holiday Inn, Maseru, 8 January 1977.
45. *LCCI*, Minutes of the Executive Committee of the Lesotho Chamber of Commerce and Industry, Victoria Hotel, Maseru, 11 June 1977.
46. *LCCI*, Minutes of the First Annual General Meeting of the Lesotho Chamber of Commerce and Industry, Victoria Hotel, Maseru, 19 March 1977.

REFERENCES

Aerni-Flessner, J. 2018. *Dreams for Lesotho: Independence, Foreign Assistance, and Development*. Notre Dame, Indiana: University of Notre Dame Press.

Ajulu, R. 1995. 'A Historical Background to Lesotho's Election of 1993', in R. Southall and T. Petlane (eds), *Democratisation and Demilitarisation in Lesotho: The General Election of 1993 and its Aftermath*. Pretoria: African Institute of South Africa, pp. 3–17.

Ferguson, J. 1994. *The Anti-Politics Machine: 'Development', Depoliticisation, and Bureaucratic Power in Lesotho*. London: University of Minnesota Press.

Freund, B. 2018. *Twentieth-Century South Africa: A Developmental History*. Cambridge: Cambridge University Press.

Hann, C., and K. Hart. 2009. 'Introduction: Learning from Polanyi 1', in C. Hann and K. Hart (eds), *Market and Society: The Great Transformation Today*. Cambridge: Cambridge University Press, pp. 1–16.

Keynes, J.M. 1936. *The General Theory of Employment, Interest and Money*. Hertfordshire: Wordsworth Editions Limited.

Khaketla, B.M. 1971. *Lesotho 1970: An African Coup under the Microscope*. London: C. Hurst & Co.

Lundahl, M., and L. Peterson. 1991. *The Dependent Economy: Lesotho and the Southern African Customs Union*. Oxford: Westview Press.

Lundahl, M., C.L. McCarthy and L. Peterson. 2003. *In the Shadow of South Africa: Lesotho's Economic Future*. Ashgate: Aldershot.

Mokuku, M. 2000. '"The Native Customers of To-day is More Intelligent than the Native Customer of a Few Years Ago": Reading the Early-Twentieth-Century Press in Colonial Lesotho', *Pretexts: Literary and Cultural Studies* 9(1): 51–62.

Montši and Associates. 1992. 'The Review of the Lesotho Chamber of Commerce and Industry's Capacity to Meet Its Mandates and Expectations', Commission Report, Ministry of Trade and Industry, Maseru.

Mphanya, N. 2010. *My Life in Basutoland Congress Party*. Maseru: Motjoli Publishers.

Ngwenya, M.A.R. 1977. 'The Nature of Basotho Owned and Managed Enterprises: A Survey of Their Constraints and Possible Promotional Measures', Commission Report, Ministry of Commerce and Industry, Maseru.

Polanyi, K. [1944] 2001. *The Great Transformation: The Political and Economic Origins of our Times*. Boston, MA: Beacon Press.

Poulter, J.A.M. 1979. *The Lesotho Law Reports: Decisions of the Court of Appeal and the High Court of Lesotho, 1971–1973*. Maseru: The Lesotho High Court.

Pule, N.W. 2002a. 'Lesotho in Southern Africa', in N.W. Pule and M. Thabane (eds), *Essays on Aspects of the Political Economy of Lesotho*. Roma: Department of History, National University of Lesotho, pp. 213–50.

———. 2002b. 'Politics since Independence', in N.W. Pule and M. Thabane (eds), *Essays on Aspects of the Political Economy of Lesotho*. Roma: Department of History, National University of Lesotho, pp. 173–212.

Ward, M. 1967. 'Economic Independence for Lesotho?', *The Journal of Modern African Studies* 5(3): 355–68.

CHAPTER 7

The Military Dictatorship and the Neoliberal Turn, 1986–2010s

Introduction

In the 1970s, a shift from the developmental model to neoliberalism began when Margaret Thatcher and Ronald Reagan pushed for economic deregulation. Neoliberal reforms focused on rolling back the state to allow for a greater role for free-market enterprise. When the Cold War ended in 1989–90, the West celebrated what it took to be the victory of capitalism; free enterprise was hailed as the uncontested engine of growth, and global capital flows were unrestricted (Hart et al. 2010: 1).

Under specific local conditions, Lesotho embraced this transition. In this chapter, I examine this shift and its circumstances. I demonstrate that a changed foreign policy and conflictual relations with South Africa over Lesotho's potential supply of water to Gauteng were central to Lesotho's adoption of Structural Adjustment Programmes (SAPs). Following perpetual disagreements over water treaty terms and conditions, South Africa simply closed its borders with Lesotho in 1986, leading to a military coup which deposed the National Party government.

The regional and international community ascribed ever-increasing poverty to the resulting dictatorship. As a consequence, it pushed for the restoration of constitutional rule and electoral politics as a drive to good governance. In 1993, the Congress Party assumed office and continued with the new IMF and World Bank market policies. Instead of addressing the country's economic challenges, we see in this chapter that these policies facilitated elitism and patronage politics, and increased economic individualism and the marginalisation of the majority. As a result, these policies aggravated poverty and inequality, and exacerbated corruption. The elites turned the state into a thiefdom and used development programmes to build a party following, while democracy and the people's own economic initiatives were neglected and marginalised.

The 1986 Coup and the Adoption of Structural Adjustment Programmes

Unsurprisingly, South Africa was not pleased with the National Party's changes in policy and international alignment after 1970 (see Chapter 6). In reprisal, it sought to destabilise Lesotho. The South African government found an ally in the dominant exiled faction of the Congress Party. Its leaders had formed the Lesotho Liberation Army (LLA), and it received support from the apartheid government (Ajulu 1995: 12–13). The Liberation Army fighters received training in Libya and Ghana before launching a series of attacks in Lesotho in 1979, in which they bombed the main post office, electricity grids, telephone posts and bridges. From 1980, the Liberation Army changed its strategy from property destruction to assassinating prominent figures in power. These activities 'forced the government to commit the country's meagre resources ever more to military-related expenditure', and 'the form of brutality that the government meted out to LLA members and suspected sympathisers made its authoritarian character pronounced and apparent' (Pule 2002: 185).

In 1985, the government announced a date for the next national election, but the Congress Party rejected the call, maintaining that the National Party regime had come to power illegitimately and that by agreeing to participate in the elections, it would be legitimising the government. The Congress Party also argued that electoral law and election participation conditions had been reformulated in ways that would favour the ruling party (Pule 2002: 187).[1]

The Congress Party made several demands. It wanted inter-party talks to be held in a foreign country, with support from the Organization of African Unity (now the African Union) or the United Nations. It also requested that the 1966 independence constitution and the 1968 electoral law be restored as the basis for negotiations, and further insisted on the formation of a coalition government, which would ensure peace and transparent preparation for elections (Pule 2002: 187). Finally, it called for the release of all political prisoners.

These demands were not all met. In addition, stringent election participation requirements led opposition parties to refuse to participate in the September elections. On 1 January 1986, the South African government closed its borders with Lesotho. South Africa justified this on the grounds that the government of Lesotho refused to expel African National Congress refugees from its territory. The South African government accused Lesotho of supporting and recruiting fighters for the military wing of the party, Umkhonto we Sizwe (Pule 2002: 187).

Lesotho began to feel the impact of the blockade, as foodstuffs and fuel supplies ran low. In January, the Lesotho Paramilitary Force surrounded the government complex and drove public servants out of their offices, in a successful move to overthrow the civilian dictatorship regime of Leabua Jonathan. Two days later, a seven-man delegation, led by Major General J.M. Lekhanya, went to Pretoria to request that the border blockade be lifted. South Africa refused. Radio Lesotho then announced that there had been a military takeover, and the blockade was immediately lifted (Machobane 2001).

The military dictatorship was worse than its civilian counterpart. It established a despotic state with widespread public harassment and looting, and it suspended political parties and collaborated with the apartheid regime. This combination made it easy for the military, in October 1986 – nine months after the coup – to sign the Lesotho Highlands Water Scheme Treaty with South Africa, without popular input. As Thabane observes: 'In Lesotho, the signing of the Highlands Water Treaty has always been associated … with the overthrow of a civilian dictatorship and its replacement by a pro-South Africa military dictatorship'. Worse, '[the] latter had even less respect for human rights and scant regard for popular opinion which enabled it to impose the Treaty on the people of Lesotho' (Thabane 2000: 634).

The signing of the treaty came after a series of earlier disagreements between Lesotho and South Africa; for a very long time, the two countries had been unable to agree on terms for its implementation. Negotiations for Lesotho to supply South Africa with water – particularly concerning the Pretoria-Witwatersrand-Vereeniging (PWV) area, now Gauteng Province – started in the 1950s. Two feasibility studies were conducted, one in the 1950s and the other in the 1960s, but they did not agree on its cost. Meanwhile, Gauteng's water needs continued to increase. In 1979, yet another feasibility study was conducted, followed by another in 1983 (Thabane 2000: 634). By this time, the Lesotho government's relations with South Africa had reached their lowest ebb.

The highlands water project had two major components: supply of water to South Africa and hydro-power plant for electricity consumption in Lesotho. South Africa was to fund the former and Lesotho the latter. Lesotho had to source funding through bilateral and multilateral borrowing from international commercial banks and other governments (Matlosa 1991: 20); to gain access to such loans, Lesotho had to acquire the International Monetary Fund's seal of approval. The IMF ensured that countries, especially so-called 'Third World' countries, were creditworthy by having them adopt Structural Adjustment Programmes (SAPs); this certified the country's ability and willingness to repay its debts. Lesotho concluded negotiations with the IMF to adopt the programmes in 1987 and implemented an austerity programme in 1988 (ibid.).

The Roots of the Neoliberal Patronage System

In 1993, Lesotho's army pulled out of government to allow for the reinstatement of a multiparty electoral system. The Congress Party finally won power. In their subsequent twenty years of government, the Congress Party implemented the rest of the privatisation reforms. Between 1993 and 2012, the country had two Prime Ministers, Ntsu Mokhehle (1993–98) and Pakalitha Mosisili (1998–2012).

With a few exceptions, the Congress Party leadership came back from exile in 1988 with the support of an impoverished people. Basotho were far from being rich, and saw the state as a goose that laid golden eggs. The party commanded incontestable electoral power – but it was deeply divided into factions. In the euphoria of demilitarisation and the transition to multiparty electoral politics, the general public did not see all this. Seduced by the allure of neoliberal reform, the party abandoned its commitment to inclusive politics: the new elite made ministries their personal fiefdoms, and the monies coming through were distributed to insiders. The cracks within the party widened, and it governed for only one term, 1993–98.

These divisions increased in the run up to the 1998 elections. Mokhehle was removed as party leader in February 1997. A breakaway faction, the Majelathoko, then formed an alternative party – the Lesotho Congress for Democracy – in June 1997 (Pule 2002: 205). The launch of the Congress for Democracy was helped by Mokhehle's popularity among ordinary party members; this was how, despite his unpopularity in the executive, he could continue politically and save the dominant Congress Party elites. The new party became the dominant party for almost fifteen years – it was built in his image, and his name was chanted like that of a god.

In May 1998, Lesotho held another general election. Three major changes were introduced in the electoral system: the voting age was reduced from 21 to 18 years; the number of constituencies was increased from sixty-five to eighty; and an Independent Electoral Commission (IEC) was formed. Before the elections, the opposition parties, mainly the Congress Party, the National Party and the Marematlou Freedom Party (MFP), applied to the High Court requesting that it postpone the election because of irregularities in the registration of voters.

In May, the High Court ruled that it did not have the power to postpone the election. The country voted on 23 May 1998. Both local and international observers agreed that the election was free and fair. The Congress for Democracy won seventy-nine out of eighty seats, while the National Party won the other one (Pule 2002: 208). The three major opposition parties challenged the results and filed petitions in the courts; when these failed, they then asked King Letsie III to dissolve the parliament and form a government of national unity. Finally, they caused a total shutdown: government offices, schools and health and other institutions were forced to close (ibid.: 209).

'Stay-aways' and seizures of government property took place; Radio Lesotho had to close, and there were frequent violent confrontations between opposition supporters and the police. These domestic conflicts culminated in external mediation by the South African Deputy President, Thabo Mbeki, resulting in the appointment of a commission of inquiry into alleged electoral irregularities in August. It was revealed that although elections had proceeded well, there had indeed been some irregularities.[2]

Meanwhile, violent confrontations between party supporters continued. The Congress for Democracy acknowledged that it had lost control and requested military assistance from the Southern African Development Community. South Africa and Botswana sent troops to Lesotho, allegedly to restore peace and order and rescue the elected government. This military intervention, in September and October, resulted in one of the most violent armed conflicts in Lesotho's recent history. As always, South Africa was the quickest to respond; they care about their water projects. I remember one morning like it was only yesterday; it was my birthday, 22 September. We were woken up by a commotion of helicopters, thundering bombs and blazing bullets. My family lives in a village close to one of the country's two military bases – the Makoanyane Military Base. The capital and other towns in the urban lowlands were severely damaged.

After the military intervention, domestic conflicts finally abated to allow for negotiations. The Congress for Democracy regained its position as leader of the government. Since 1966, the country had used the 'First Past the Post' electoral system, and politicians criticised this for excluding 'from parliament parties with a sizeable following and [promoted] a culture of disputing and contesting election results' (Mothibe 2017: 67). To address previous political failures, the government established an Interim Political Authority in 1998 to design a suitable electoral model. The Authority established a Mixed Member Proportional Representation system.

The events of 1998 affected Lesotho's economy negatively, especially for ordinary people. Many felt that food aid would have to be made generally available. Retail and wholesale businesses were the most severely damaged, since they had been burnt and raided for food supplies. Over a thousand businesses, mostly Basotho-owned, were damaged countrywide; these were small retail shops, butcheries, bakeries, cosmetics and hair salons, and footwear and clothing shops (Makhetha 2008).

About 80 per cent of damaged Basotho businesses were owned by women. Of the total, almost eight hundred were in Maseru, and over one hundred each in Mafeteng and Mohale's Hoek.[3] Damages were valued at millions of South African rands (Makhetha 2008). Two-thirds of the Basotho businesses in Maseru reopened by the year's end, and a small number of damaged businesses resumed operations in the districts of Mafeteng (36 per cent) and Mohale's Hoek (23 per cent). Over four hundred businesses, employing two thousand people, never resumed trading.

Neoliberal Reforms, Elitism and Exclusion

Now uncontested, the Lesotho Congress for Democracy continued to implement neoliberal reforms. However, the Congress government, along with informal elites, maintained control of the economic opportunities that came with Lesotho's neoliberal transition for their own ends. They used political power and influence to distribute these opportunities to a few business groups, consisting of selected party members, fellow politicians, foreign investors, friends and family. Consequently, the majority of Basotho business owners were excluded from the economic benefits of restructuring. The government deliberately frustrated and fragmented Basotho business by employing 'divide-and-rule' strategies; rewarding those who followed its dictates while sidelining those who challenged its authority. The government's authoritarian rule relied more on corruption than that of its predecessor.

Lesotho's Structural Adjustment Programmes came in three packages: the first set from 1988/89 to 1990/91, the second from 1991/92 to 1994/95 and the last from 1995 to 2000. The second and the last programmes were called the Enhanced Structural Adjustment Facility and the Privatization and Private Sector Development Project respectively. These programmes were implemented by the Congress Party government when it assumed power in 1993.[4] The Congress Party government and the World Bank implemented the first five-year phase of the Lesotho Privatization and Private Sector Development Programme in 1995. Its main aim was to:

> free taxpayers of subsidies to non-performing state enterprises, to attract capitalization and management expertise, [to] stimulate growth, efficiency and job creation [as well as] to create a favourable climate for private sector development.[5]

As a result, state-owned companies were privatised.[6] To facilitate the country's privatisation and economic reconstruction programme, the government passed the Privatization Act No. 9 of 1995. This did two major things: first, the government established the Lesotho Privatization Unit under the Ministry of Finance, to 'plan, manage, implement and control the privatization process';[7] second, it laid down privatisation principles, guidelines and regulations to be followed. Three methods were adopted: private management contracts; the outright sale of company shares and/or their assets; and liquidation of bankrupt companies and parastatals.[8]

From the outset, the government excluded ordinary Basotho from owning shares in the state-owned companies to be privatised. It justified this on the grounds that there were no regulations guiding public issuance of shares to domestic companies. It also argued that because Basotho did not have the requisite capacity (that is, the skills and money), they should not be allowed to own shares in such companies. The government then gave the responsibility for investment in newly privatised companies to the Lesotho Development National Corporation, through Lesotho Investment Holdings, which had been created in 1991.[9] It affirmed that:

> The declared policy objective of GoL (Government of Lesotho) is to avail the indigenous private sector an opportunity to effectively and profitably participate in economic activities in the country. However, the lack of business culture in Lesotho and absence of a viable mechanism for enabling the indigenous business community to buy shares in profitable business ventures call for the need for selective and cautious disinvestment from the existing portfolio of profitable and mature LNDC companies.[10]

As a corollary, the government created Business Advisory and Promotion Services in 1992 to work in collaboration with the World Bank to help prepare Indigenously owned businesses to take control of the local economy at a later stage. This organisation was mandated to assist with the development of Indigenous businesses through the provision of business skills and technical advice.[11] It was also supported, financially and technically, by Ireland, Germany and the United States Agency for International Development, with the latter two focusing on agricultural businesses.[12]

The government removed the credit-lending portfolio of the Basotho Enterprises Development Corporation in 1993 and transferred it to the Lesotho Bank.[13] The mandates of the older enterprise-development institutions were subsequently narrowed to training Basotho and mentoring them to develop 'bankable business plans'. The government claimed that: 'There was excess liquidity with the commercial banks mainly because the banks do not get viable proposals'.[14] Notwithstanding all this, the majority never laid a finger on this alleged excess liquidity (Lesotho Cooperative College 1990: 8). Many business loan applications made by Basotho were turned down by bank officials, who claimed that their proposals were not 'bankable' and they did not have collateral.

As Basotho were struggling to get credit from the banks, top government officials, and their friends and family members, had easier access to business loans. In an interview with one business owner and former senior employee of the Lesotho Bank (later Agric-Bank), I was told that bank managers would request that they approve certain business loan applications from high-ranking government officials and their friends, even if they did not meet the bank's conditions.[15] The informant revealed:

> The banks at the time also had political issues. I have a very difficult personality to deal with. I don't just agree to something when I realise that it is not proper. [A person would] just be given a loan of half a million. [That person] does not qualify, you are instructed to process the loan and I wouldn't do it … I decided to say, okay fine, I am leaving. I left the bank.

The government created two programmes due to 'major public criticisms of the Lesotho Privatization and Private Sector Development' – criticisms alleging especially that Basotho had 'not been afforded the opportunity to purchase shares of former state-owned enterprises'.[16] First, it created the Entrepreneurship Training Programme in 1996, which was placed under the Basotho Enterprises Development Corporation. This programme operated with minimal success until 2000, having been established because the Business Advisory and Promotion Services had 'not performed as excepted'.[17]

Second, the government launched the Lesotho Unit Trust in August 2001. The Unit Trust was an investment holding through which interested and capable Basotho could together buy shares in privatised companies. The government established the Standard Bank Unit Trust (Pty) Ltd to manage the Trust privately. In an example of affirmative action, the government's Lesotho Unit Trust Bill of 2003 gave the Trust a number of tax exemptions and subsidies in order to increase returns on investments for Basotho investors.[18] The main objective of the Bill was to 'make provision for administration, investment and management of the Lesotho Unit Trust', with the aim to 'accord … concession and subsidies that will make the Trust an attractive investment opportunity of the citizens of Lesotho'.[19]

Consolidating Congress Economic Power: The Lesotho Smart Partnership Hub

In its fifteen years of government, the Lesotho Congress for Democracy centralised and tightly controlled economic opportunities to consolidate its power. It established the Lesotho Smart Partnership Hub as a decisive step in this direction. Congress officials, fellow party members, and friends and family had a stake in virtually all lucrative sectors of the economy, including mining, shopping malls, health, tourism, education, Lesotho Highlands Water Projects, construction and civil works, professional services, airlines and agriculture. It was an unwritten law of the party that with support from a trusted official, an individual could obtain almost anything, from a position to a tender, upon producing a party membership card. The new elite also aligned itself with foreign investors.

In 2005, the government launched the Hub with the rationale of creating 'dialogue' between the business community and the government. As outlined by the Lesotho Smart Partnership Chapter, it sought to counter the following problems: red tape and theft, lack of consultation between government and business, government delays in payment of service providers, poor dissemination of government information, high tax rates, lack of transparency at the Central Tender Board, preferential treatment of foreign companies by the government, lack of local entrepreneurship skills and discrimination based on politics, gender and religion.[20]

The Smart Partnership was an idea adopted from Malaysia during the leadership of President Mahathir bin Mohamad, who is credited with championing it as an economic strategy in that country.[21] In 1995, the Smart Partnership was established in New Zealand, as a movement in some Commonwealth countries. The idea behind it was to bring various economic spheres together with the aim of exchanging information, ideas, interests and experiences in the pursuit of a vibrant economy. It was organised around eight groups, called the 'Links' in Smart Partnership terminology: Government and Politics, Social Issues, Labour, Media, Academia, Arts and Culture, Business and Club 29 (Youth). People would join these various groups depending on their interests and skills.[22]

When it was launched in Lesotho, the Hub was placed directly under the Prime Minister's Office, ensuring that it enjoyed generous financial and political support from both the government and international institutions. For example, in the financial year 2011/12, the government received a total of R1.8 billion in the form of loans and grants from various development partners, including the European Investment Bank, the World Bank, the Saudi Fund for Development, the Organization of the Petroleum Exporting Countries (OPEC), the Multilateral Debt Relief Initiative, Irish Aid, the European Union (EU), the African Development Bank (ADB) and the IMF.[23]

In 2005–2012, its active years, the Hub made several significant contributions to the economy and business infrastructure. I will provide three examples to substantiate this point. First, in 2009, the Hub pushed for the establishment of what is called the One-Stop Business Facilitation Centre (OBFC), popularly called the One-Stop Shop, under the Ministry of Trade, Industry, Co-operatives and Marketing.[24] The One-Stop Shop brought together under one roof various Ministries and Authorities involved in issuing licences, company registration, import and export permits, visas, tax clearances and resident permits, to ensure easy access to these business services.[25]

Second, the public and government persistently criticised institutions of higher learning in Lesotho for providing a curriculum that did not support the needs of the country, and those of business in particular. For instance, the government held that Lesotho's '[v]ocational training outfits … do not appear to meet the skills requirements of the established industries'.[26] Accordingly, the government and the Hub worked towards the establishment of the Limkokwing University of Creative Technology in 2008.[27] This is a private tertiary institution, owned by Tan Sri Dato, Sri Paduka and Dr Lim Kok Wing and with its headquarters in Malaysia.

The new university was established in such a short time that it immediately sparked numerous controversies. Many government buildings were rented out to it, while students who could not qualify for enrolment at the National University of Lesotho (at the time the only university in the country) and other reputable institutions of higher learning were accepted in large numbers. These students were funded by the government to pursue their studies ('University of Cash and Tosh' 2011). As it turned out, the qualifications students obtained were not recognised by numerous international and national institutions of higher learning. In September 2012, the Council on Higher Education[28] called for a commission of inquiry into the operations and qualifications of Limkokwing University. The Ministry of Education ignored this and kept quiet. *Lesotho Times*, a local newspaper, reported: 'Basotho are a resilient people, but they were shattered to discover that, as an investment, Limkokwing is something of a Ponzi scheme' ('University of Cash and Tosh' 2011).

Third, the Hub launched the Business Council of Lesotho in October 2009. The main purpose of the Council was to create dialogue specifically between the government and the business community. It was first proposed in a Smart Partnership Hub gathering in 2006.[29] The Council consisted of representatives of the business community (the Business Foundation) and of the government, and was chaired by the Prime Minister. It sat only six times between its formation and 2012, when the Prime Minister, Pakalitha Mosisili, lost elections to a coalition of opposition parties (see Chapter 9).[30] The Council ensured that the Prime Minister and his allies had absolute control over the economy and business.

Lastly, the Smart Partnership, in collaboration with the Business Council, successfully pushed for the formation of a Partial Credit Guarantee Scheme in November 2011, to help aspiring Basotho entrepreneurs to gain access to capital. The scheme was placed under the Lesotho National Development Corporation. It was launched to give access to finance to people who wish to start or expand medium to large-size businesses without adequate collateral. The scheme provided a 50 per cent guarantee on loans ranging from R200,000 to R5 million.[31]

The corporation's official, Raleche Semethe, made the startling observation that in Lesotho, 'access to finance [was] the major inhibiting factor'. Semethe added: 'local banks are hesitant to broaden their services to aid businesses in Lesotho … the local business framework is such that 15% are large Basotho-owned businesses while the remaining bulk (or 85%) are small businesses', and these businesses 'need to be supported financially to grow larger … if the banks hesitate to boost them financially'.[32]

Three banks were identified as partners in the credit scheme: South Africa's Ned Bank, Standard Bank and First National Bank. Applications were made to both the development corporation and these banks. Through the scheme, the government would provide 50 per cent as indemnity for all loans. The scheme focused on the following business sectors: agro-processing, mining and quarrying, tourism, information technology, construction, franchising and manufacturing. After almost a year, only three people had gained access to the money. Only R1.8 million of the allocated R10 million had been used by 2012, when the Congress regime collapsed.[33]

Summary

The restoration of constitutional rule in 1993 was a highly anticipated moment in the contemporary history of Lesotho. Like the dictatorships preceding it, however, the Congress government used development intervention to enrich a few elitist groups in the economy. Prime Minister

Mosisili's approach to governance was strategically authoritarian, and among his methods of repression, he deployed force only sparingly. He centralised resources around his office and political party, generously rewarding those that followed his dictates.

This approach deepened poverty and inequality in the tiny mountain kingdom. Competition over meagre resources escalated internal conflicts and the struggle for office. Corruption became the order of the day; political parties became the primary means to access resources and opportunities, instead of facilitating a representative role to advance democratic ideals and social justice.

Furthermore, and as this chapter has demonstrated, the Congress abandoned its historic mission to work for the poor and advance their economic interests. In the run-up to independence and immediately after, it charismatically combined commerce and co-operativism in order to negotiate favourable conditions with South Africa for the Basotho, turning away from its political manifesto of opening talks with South Africa on 'Conquered Territories' and finding possible ways to reclaim Basotho lands.

NOTES

1. Indeed, smaller opposition parties – in particular, the South Africa-funded Basotho Democratic Alliance – attempted to contest the elections, but were unable to meet the required conditions. The South African government's efforts to destabilise and eventually topple the National Party government were not only limited to military tactics; they also included an open political strategy of assisting in the formation of a political party which would contest elections.
2. *Transformation Resource Centre*, 'The Report of the Commission of Enquiry into the Conduct and Results of the Lesotho General Elections held in May 1998', 9 September 1998.
3. *LCCI*, Lesotho 1998: Assessment of Damages to Business and Loss of Employment Report – A Joint Assessment of 1,045 Businesses in Maseru and District Towns, November 1998.
4. *LNA, Ministry of Trade and Industry Documents, MTI/DEV/SAF/12/104/Vol. 1*, Enhanced Structural Adjustments Facility; 'First Lesotho Privatization and Private Sector Development Project Progress (1995–2002)'. Retrieved 14 May 2014 from http://lesothoembassy.de/PUweb/documents/progress-rpt-9502.htm.
5. 'Fourth Annual Report: Lesotho Privatization and Private Sector Development Project,1 April 1999 to 31 March 2000'. Retrieved 13 May 2014 from Lesothoembassy.de/PUweb/projects/Privatised.htm.
6. 'First Lesotho Privatization and Private Sector Development Project Progress (1995–2002)'. Retrieved 14 May 2014 from http://lesothoembassy.de/PUweb/documents/progress-rpt-9502.htm.

7. Ibid.
8. Ibid.
9. *LNA, Ministry of Trade Documents, MTV/DEV/SAF/12/104/Vol. 1*, Notes for Discussion on 25 October 1991 for the IMF Mission visiting Lesotho from 20 October 1991 to 12 November 1991 for the Mid-term Review of Enhanced Structural Adjustment Facility (ESAF): Government Policy Framework Paper for the Period 1991/92, 1992/93, 1993/94, April 1991.
10. Ibid.
11. *LNA, Ministry Trade Documents, MTV/DEV/SAF/12/104/Vol. 1*, Enhanced Structural Adjustment Facility Conditionality Report.
12. *LNA, Ministry of Trade Documents, MTV/DEV/SAF/12/104/Vol. 1*, A Concept Paper for 1994/95, ESAP Successor Negations.
13. *LNA, Ministry of Trade Documents, T&I/DEV/6/2/Vol. 1*, Plans for the Restructuring of BEDCO.
14. *LNA, Ministry of Trade Documents, MTV/DEV/SAF/12/104/Vol. 1*, IMF Task-Force Midterm Review of E.S.A.F Meeting, Ministry of Planning, 11 March 1994, Maseru.
15. Lesotho Bank was liquidated in 1999.
16. *Annual Report: Lesotho Privatization and Private Sector Development Project (1997–1998)*. Retrieved 13 May 2014 from Lesothoembassy.de/PUweb/projects/Privatised.htm.
17. Ibid.
18. Lesotho Parliamentary Debates (*Hansard*), Fifth Meeting, Sixth Session, 4 September 2003.
19. Ibid., 22.
20. *A Report on Lesotho National Business Dialogue*, 'Manthabiseng Convention Centre, Maseru, Lesotho, 5–6 April 2006, 12.
21. *Smart Partnership: Southern African International Dialogue Proceedings Report*, Maseru, Lesotho, 9–12 November 2005, 1.
22. Ibid.
23. Progress Report distributed during the National Dialogue in Preparation for the Global 2013 Smart Partnership Conference, Maseru Sun Hotel, Maseru, Lesotho, 29 May 2013.
24. *A Report on Lesotho National Business Dialogue*, 'Manthabiseng Convention Centre, Maseru, Lesotho, 5–6 April 2006, 12.
25. 'One-Stop Business Facilitation Centre'. 2014. Retrieved 13 May 2013 from http://www.obfc.org.ls/aboutUs/default.php.
26. 'Small States in Transition – From Vulnerability to Competitiveness'. 2004. Retrieved 2 March 2014 from www.intracen.org/WorkArea/DownloadAsset.aspx?id=52379.
27. Interview with Lira Ralese, Director of Smart Partnership Hub (2006–2012), Maseru, 25 June 2013.
28. The Council was established in 2004 to regulate education in Lesotho's institutions of higher learning and to ensure its quality.
29. *A Report on Lesotho National Business Dialogue*, 'Manthabiseng Convention Centre, Maseru, Lesotho, 5–6 April 2006, 12.

30. *LCCI*, Prime Minister's Office letter of invitation to the Lesotho Chamber of Commerce and Industry to be part of the Business Council, 22 February 2013; Minutes of the Meeting between the Principle Secretary of the Ministry of Trade and Industry with the Lesotho Chamber of Commerce and Industry, LCCI Head Office, Maseru, 19 March 2013.
31. 'Lesotho Launches M50 Million Partial Credit Guarantee Fund'. Retrieved 15 August 2020 from http://lestimes.com/lesotho-launches-m50million-partial-credit-guarantee-fund/.
32. 'Lesotho Partial Credit Scheme'. 2014. Retrieved 14 May 2014 from http://www.lndc.org.ls/services/PCG-Pilot.php.
33. 'Lesotho Launches M50 Million Partial Credit Guarantee Fund'. Retrieved 15 August 2020 from http://lestimes.com/lesotho-launches-m50million-partial-credit-guarantee-fund/.

REFERENCES

Ajulu, R. 1995. 'A Historical Background to Lesotho's Election of 1993', in R. Southall and T. Petlane (eds), *Democratisation and Demilitarisation in Lesotho: The General Election of 1993 and its Aftermath*. Pretoria: African Institute of South Africa, pp. 3–17.

Hart, K., J. Laville and A.D. Cattani. 2010. 'Building the Human Economy Together', in K. Hart, J. Laville and A.D. Cattani (eds), *The Human Economy: A Citizen's Guide*. Cambridge: Polity Press, pp. 1–17.

Lesotho Cooperative College. 1990. 'Small Business Education and Training Report', *Lesotho Cooperative College Seminar*, Maseru, 18–22 June 1990. Maseru, Lesotho Cooperative College.

Machobane, L.B.B.J. 2001. *The King's Knights: Military Governance in the Kingdom of Lesotho, 1986–1993*. Roma: Institute of Southern African Studies.

Makhetha, M. 2008. 'The Socio-Economic Cost of the Post-Election Conflict', *Journal of African Elections: Special Issue – Elections and Democracy in Lesotho* 7(1): 153–63.

Matlosa, K. 1991. 'Structural Adjustment Programmes and the Employment Challenge in Lesotho', *South African Political and Economic Monthly* 4(7): 16–28.

Mothibe, T. 2017. 'Political Leadership Challenge in Lesotho – A Cause of Political Instability', in M. Thabane (ed.), *Towards an Anatomy of Persistent Political Instability in Lesotho, 1966–2016*. Roma: National University of Lesotho, pp. 47–73.

Pule, N.W. 2002. 'Politics since Independence', in N.W. Pule and M. Thabane (eds), *Essays on Aspects of the Political Economy of Lesotho*. Roma: Department of History, National University of Lesotho, pp. 173–212.

Thabane, M. 2000. 'Shifts from Old to New Social and Ecological Environments in the Lesotho Highlands Water Scheme: Relocating Residents of the Mohale Dam Area', *Journal of Southern African Studies* 26(4): 633–54.

'University of Cash and Tosh'. 2011. *Lesotho Times*, 28 December 2011. Retrieved 14 February 2015 from http://lestimes.com/university-of-cash-and-tosh.

CHAPTER 8

Business Politics and the Collapse of the Congress, 2000s–2020

Introduction

With the dawn of the present century, inequality in Lesotho increased significantly. The neoliberal turn facilitated and justified patronage politics, elitism and the exclusion of the masses; Basotho were neglected and marginalised. The Congress had long ago abandoned its historic mission to pursue democracy 'in any meaningful sense' with the interests of the poor in the forefront. In the words of Hart et al.:

> We have just been through a prolonged social experiment in which markets and money were left to find their own way around the world ... This experiment has been called 'neoliberalism' ... The freedom of these markets was mainly for those with lots of money. The rest of us had to adjust; and society became much more unequal as a result. One victim of neoliberalism was certainly democracy in any meaningful sense. (2010: 1)

I advance in this chapter, however, that the people were not passive victims of the Congress's authoritarianism and its exclusionary economic policies. Under unfavourable conditions, they made what they could of the local economy and became more politically active. This century's first decade saw waves of popular unrest and strikes. Under the leadership of the Chamber of Commerce and other trade unions, the business community played a leading role in the fight against the government's divisive policies.

Business community members had been some of the first to feel the impact of neoliberal patronage politics, and then displacement by Chinese traders. By the 2010s, their political activities had contributed to erosion of the Congress movement's legitimacy and coherence. Prime Minister Pakalitha Mosisili's fifteen-year reign came to an end in 2012; thereafter, the country suffered a series of unstable and violent coalition governments (see Thabane 2017; Sejanamane 2017).

Resistance from the Chamber of Commerce

After 1993, relations between the Chamber of Commerce and the Congress Party government were amicable. Although the Chamber's membership was mixed in terms of political parties, the bulk was composed of non-exiled members of the Congress Party. The Chamber bought Security Lesotho Ltd Pty when the privatisation reforms began. When the Lesotho Congress for Democracy took over government following the 1998 elections, it gave the Chamber a site to build offices. The Chamber found developers to finance the office complex, and rented out unused sections to repay its debts.

In return, the government used the Chamber to consolidate its control over the local economy and business.[1] Relations between the two changed for the worse in the early 2000s when the Chamber maintained its pro-Basotho position instead of simply dancing to the government's tune. An influential group of Maseru-based members approached Simon Kuena Phafane, whom they had learned to respect, to lead the Chamber. This is when the rift occurred.

Phafane was the former Personal Assistant to Moshoeshoe II (Lesotho's king from 1966 to 1996), as well as Principal Secretary of the Ministry of Trade, Commerce and Industry and former Chief Executive Officer of the Basotho Enterprises Development Corporation. He was an ideal person to rescue the Chamber from its political crisis. Members campaigned around the country to install him as the leader of the Chamber. In 2003, he became Deputy President, and in 2005 he was elected as President.[2]

As leader, Phafane was vocal in his criticism of the government's undemocratic control of the local economy. He refused to take orders from the government. Phafane's view was that: 'The guy who had been elected President was very weak. He would go to the Minister of Trade … He'd go to him and get instructions to tell us what to do'. Phafane added: 'Maseru [branch] resisted that, and I also felt no, we can't be dictated ... to do certain things by the Minister'.[3] The Chamber even questioned the undemocratic implications of the Prime Minister's position as chair of the Business Council. 'Mammako Molapo, a member of the Chamber, said:

> I was one of the people who were fighting very hard saying that I do not understand how it is that the Business Council can be started and [the government can claim that] it [was] the mother body, yet there was Lesotho Chamber of Commerce and Industry, as the mother body. And, if the Lesotho Chamber of Commerce and Industry had problems and weaknesses [that] we saw, why [did they] not strengthen [it]? [Instead] another body [was] formed [by the government]. Why do people have to be divided? I [didn't']

> understand why … and I really refused that the Chamber should join that thing. I was saying, 'let us be given an explanation as to why the Business Council [was] formed'. I'm [also] one of the people who were saying 'I don't agree that the Prime Minister [should] be the chairman of the body.[4]

The government retaliated by supporting the Mohloli Chamber of Business (later just Mohloli), which became influential in the Smart Partnership Hub. The Chamber of Commerce was marginalised and came to be viewed as an incapable organisation, ridden with petty politics and composed of insignificant, regressive Basotho business owners.[5] Mohloli was formed by a group of Basotho business owners in December 2005; at its core were five business owners who had close economic relations to King Letsie III. The group called itself Sesiu ('the granary'). Earlier in 2005, one of their friends had died, with neither the resources nor the family support to facilitate a burial. The partners approached the King for assistance, and the King advised them to establish an organisation that would help them in the long term.[6]

At first, they had thought of approaching the Chamber to carry out their idea. At the time, however, it had many internal conflicts, so they decided instead to establish an organisation of their own, following the king's advice. Mohloli immediately became a powerful economic force in Lesotho. It attracted a lot of public attention by drawing in rich Basotho business owners, and it formed strong relations with the government.[7]

It did not survive for long, however, collapsing in 2008 for political reasons. In 2006, a group of members of the ruling party, dissatisfied with the Prime Minister's authoritarian style of leadership, had formed a political party called the All-Basotho Convention (ABC), under the leadership of Thomas Thabane. In the run-up to the 2008 elections, competition between the government and the new party for power and influence spilled over into Mohloli, and the organisation's leadership and membership split between these two political parties. Thuso Green, former Deputy President of the association, acknowledges this:

> We failed to be neutral and take a business line when it came to political issues in 2008 … that is where the trouble began. Some within us stood for the elections … everybody was thinking that ABC was going to make it and ABC was 'the thing' in politics … that's where the crash of Mohloli came. Then people started saying 'we have to change the chairperson because we think he is an ABC member [and all sorts of things] … At that stage … we started having problems [and it collapsed].[8]

After Mohloli's collapse, the government established the Private Sector Foundation of Lesotho (PSFL, later just the Foundation) in 2009, with assistance from the World Bank.[9] It justified its formation by maintaining that Basotho business owners lacked the spirit of co-operation and unity required to deal effectively with their problems in the local economy. Thus, they could not play an effective role in the development of local business.

As further punishment, the government withdrew the subvention fund from the Chamber of Commerce. This was calculated at 20 per cent of all national licencing fees paid per year. The government claimed that the Chamber could no longer be given the subvention since there were other associations representing different segments of the business community.[10] The Chamber questioned and challenged this withdrawal, but to no avail. The Prime Minister responded:

> The Lesotho Chamber of Commerce and Industry (LCCI) lost its right to receive funding from government because it no longer represents all trade associations ... other associations of equal standing had come on board ... Today industry has grown and widened and there are many business associations and therefore LCCI no longer represents all businesses … the money is now being given to the Private Sector Foundation 'which represents all trade associations' … LCCI and other similar associations must join the Private Sector Foundation to access funding ... The LCCI is making itself miserable by keeping itself detached from talks between traders and the government. We cannot cry for someone who caused himself problems.[11]

The ruling party began to use the new entity as its vehicle to control Lesotho's economic development and business initiatives, and its activities and membership remained largely centralised in the capital. It was not long before the Foundation started to show signs of hidden political and economic interests. Evidence began to emerge from 2011, when it had internal conflicts. One of its leaders, Leonia Mosothoane, showed that: '[S]ince its establishment in 2009, there had never been transparency among the board members … there was a lot of favouritism' (Tlali 2012). During these conflicts, a notable example of shady dealing and political privilege emerged via the exposure and conviction of Osman Moosa, the Foundation's chairman, for fraud and tax evasion. In August 2011, Moosa and his son were found guilty of 361 counts of fraud and tax evasion. They were ordered by the High Court to pay a total of R6.1 million in fines and taxes to the Lesotho Revenue Authority (ibid.).

By the late 2000s, the business community was highly fragmented, with the Private Sector Foundation positioned as the darling of the government. The government's rule was simple: You are either with us or against us. The government frustrated and divided the local business community. The impact was felt even by smaller associations that depended on the associations at the top. Without subvention funds, the Chamber found it difficult to carry out its activities and support affiliated associations, and it lost a large part of its membership to the newly formed and well-resourced Private Sector Foundation. Tsietsi Chabatsane, chair of the Leribe Forestry Association and the Leribe branch of the Chamber, said: 'The reason why we join LCN [the Lesotho Council of Non-Governmental Organizations], the Chamber and other associations is that we are looking for support ... That is why we complain that the Chamber is not doing anything for us'.[12] These associations knew little of boardroom politics in the capital. Various Basotho business groups began forming alternative associations as they seceded from the Chamber for self-preservation; among the most notable were the Mafeteng Chamber of Business and Theko 'Moho.[13]

In 2011, the Lesotho Revenue Authority (LRA), with assistance from the Southern African Development Community (SADC), initiated a business forum – the Lesotho Revenue Authority Business Partnership Forum, hereafter just the Forum.[14] Its vision was to provide direction and foster unity within the business community. It was to be a platform through which all business associations would share their collective concerns, irrespective of their associational affiliations. At first, the Chamber of Commerce was part of this arrangement. When the Forum was launched, however, its structures resembled those of any other business association. The Chamber withdrew its participation as a result.[15] The Forum was subsequently joined by members of the business community who were exasperated with business politics. However, it was short-lived; by 2013, it was moribund.

From the mid-2000s, the local business community had already begun to fragment; it lacked direction and focus owing to the Congress government's authoritarianism, based on the maxims of 'divide and rule' and 'reward and punishment'. This approach sparked widespread discontent and protests.

The Coalition of Concerned Citizens and the 'Mother of all Protests'

Congress's authoritarianism effectively created its own countermovement. As a result, the 2000s were characterised by a series of protests coming from different spheres of the economy. The business associations, factory workers, tertiary students, youth organisations, teachers' unions, informal street traders, transport associations and various sections of civil society all made petitions. Needless to say, their efforts were repressed; the government acted violently against their protests and leadership. What follow here are some highlights of the formation of a solidarity movement, leading to the national shutdown in August 2011 under the leadership of the Chamber of Commerce and the Maseru Regional Taxi Organization (MRTO, hereafter just the Taxi Organization).

To begin with, the Factory Workers' Union (FAWU), the Lesotho Clothing and Allied Workers Union (LECAWU) and the National Union of Textile Workers (NUTEX) fought for the wages and working conditions of factory and low-skilled workers. The government ignored their grievances and suppressed their protests ('Lesotho Unions Merge' 2015; International Labour Organisation 2012). In 1980, foreign direct investment (FDI) contributed 1.2 per cent to the country's GDP. In 1985, this had increased to 8.5 per cent, reaching 25 per cent by 1990. By the 2000s, it had quadrupled (Ministry of Finance and Development Planning 2004).

The cornerstone of the government's strategy was the textile and garments manufacturing industry. This contributed significantly to the country's economy and employment. The industry was given a further boost when Lesotho qualified in 2000 for the African Growth and Opportunity Act (AGOA) (Manoeli 2012; Shakya 2011). As a result, the textiles industry went from employing around fifteen thousand people in 2000 to employing some fifty thousand by 2007 (Shakya 2011: 221). Exploitation and human-rights abuses, however, are notorious features of this industry (Manoeli 2012: 3).

In 2008, the government bought twenty buses in an attempt to undercut private taxi and bus operators' 'stay-aways' – interruptions of service intended to allow the operators, not the government, to determine their fares. Led by the Taxi Organization, taxi operators staged a strike and blocked roads in May when the new government fleet first came into operation. The police were ordered to clear them off using rifles and tear gas (United States Federal Government 2010).

In 2009, the Chamber launched the Junior Chamber International to advance the interests of young professionals and entrepreneurs and to combat brain-drain and high unemployment. The Junior Chamber International immediately supported resistance against the Business Council and the Partial Credit Scheme. Instead of the credit scheme controlled by the government, it argued that a board consisting of various stakeholders (including government, business, civil society and associations) should control the scheme for wider inclusion and transparency.[16]

In December 2010, street traders in Maseru were up in arms against the City Council's efforts to forcefully relocate them from their lucrative spaces. As part of its clean-up operation, the City Council argued that the vendors' occupation was illegal, and that they were using their businesses as brothels and drinking houses (*shebeens*). As Setšabi and Leduka, locally based urban-development scholars, have argued: 'Behind the facade of public health and urban aesthetics as reasons for the eviction of street traders lies overt exercise of state power to protect the interests of formal sector businesses' in attempts to 'disguise state failure to formulate inclusive and sustainable urban policies' (2008: 221).

From the mid-2000s, the government systematically reduced funding and support to the National University of Lesotho. This kept the Lesotho University Teachers and Researchers Union (LUTARU) busy with petitions, but their efforts were to no avail. During the 2011 academic year, the government and management significantly reduced student enrolments. In June, the Congress of Lesotho Trade Unions (COLETU), the Lesotho Teachers Trade Union (LTTU), the Journalists Union of Lesotho (JUL) and the Lesotho College of Education Union (LCEU) marched in solidarity with the teachers, researchers and students, against the university management and the government.[17]

In 2011, these trade unions and business organisations changed their approach; instead of protesting on their own, they united and fought together. Organised and led by the Chamber and the Taxi Organization, Basotho formed a solidarity movement against the Prime Minister called the 'Coalition of Concerned Citizens'. The movement had two distinctive characteristics. Firstly, it 'was the first one to have pulled a crowd that represented more than just political parties and special interest groups' in Lesotho's history ('Lesotho: Nation's Mother of All Protests' 2011). The local media labelled it the 'Mother of all Protests'. Secondly, and in addition to its broad composition, the Coalition made demands that went beyond typical trade-union petitions for better wages, improved working conditions and favourable economic opportunities, or challenging election outcomes.[18] Mokete Jonase, a taxi driver and chair of the Maseru Regional Taxi Organisation, said:

> It is a new dawn in the citizens' patriotism and consciousness in Lesotho … elections have not solved the problems and therefore people should not wait for elections in the hope that they will change the government but should hold the present government accountable. It is time for the poor to fight for their rights that have been trampled upon by the rich. (Ibid.)

After a three-day 'stay-away' from 15 August, the protesters marched to the Prime Minister's office on August 23. Their demands included the following: government accountability; better service delivery; the improvement of the legal system (and not just for the rich); increases in taxi fares; higher salaries for factory workers; that the Prime Minister step down as chair of the Business Council; protection of Indigenously owned businesses from the Chinese and other foreign business interests; that civil servants be allowed to form or join unions; the cutting down of the Prime Minister and Cabinet's luxurious benefits; free cross-border movement of Basotho to other countries; and that the government take up again the restoration of the 'Conquered Territories' – land appropriated from Lesotho by the Afrikaners in the nineteenth century (see Chapter 2).[19]

Unsurprisingly, the Prime Minister avoided addressing the protesters and their grievances. Instead, the government cut from the air four private radio stations that supported and broadcast the August events; 'only static could be heard from the four stations' frequencies'.[20] The radio stations were People's Choice FM, MoAfrika FM, Harvest FM and Thaha-Khube FM (ibid.; 'Lesotho: Nation's Mother of All Protests' 2011). 'Malichaba Lekhoaba, the manager of Harvest FM, was summoned by the Acting Principal Secretary of the Ministry of Communications and the Chief Executive Officer of Lesotho Communications Authority, who threatened to shut down the radio stations if they did not 'mend their ways, as this was a sensitive issue'. Lekhoaba was informed that the government considered their coverage to be 'disrespectful'.[21]

The government said that the four radio stations had closed down as a result of 'technical failures', but everyone knew that this was a cover-up.[22] The government made sure that the rest of the country was kept in the dark about the movement's activities. The movement's leaders, however, maintained that in their view the movement had succeeded, particularly by putting pressure on the government and in expressing the people's common grievances. It had become difficult for people to freely express their discontent with the government. The representative of the Chamber, 'Malitlou Morojele – who was a Mosotho businesswoman, one of the prominent leaders of the movement and Chair of the Maseru Chamber of Commerce and Industry at the time – was clear:

> We realised that the ruling party does not have an ear. There was nothing going well in the country. The taxi men came and said: 'No, Mrs Morojele, we cannot sit down and watch these things which are happening in our country' … I was part of the leadership which made that march … we were saying 'no', as the business community. We were saying 'no' to the Chinese – 'no' to many things … I will always say [that] the things we did were a success. I believe such a protest has never been seen in this country.[23]

Calling for change and a general will to persevere, one of the movement's leaders, Manama Letsie, was vehement: 'We will not end our struggle. We will fight until we achieve what we are demanding. We will not even run away from this country; we will face everything and everyone head-on. What we need is change' ('Lesotho: Nation's Mother of All Protests 2011').

The Overthrow of Mosisili and the End of the Congress Movement

After the 'Mother of All Protests', Lesotho held general elections in the following May, in a storm of 'Anti-Prime Minister' sentiment. People desperately needed change, particularly in urban areas. In February 2012, a few days before parliament closed in preparation for the election, forty-five Members of Parliament from the Lesotho Congress for Democracy crossed the floor. This splinter group formed the Democratic Congress (DC). This followed conflict between two major factions in the LCD: these were the 'Lija-Mollo' ('fire eaters'), who supported the Prime Minister, and the 'Litima-Mollo' (fire extinguishers), who supported the party's Secretary-General, Mothejoa Metsing, who subsequently became the new leader of the Congress for Democracy (Letsie 2013: 65–67).

In the same parliamentary session, the Speaker, Ntlhoi Motsamai, declared the Democratic Congress to be the government, despite it not having two-thirds of the 120 seats. According to the Constitution, such a party can form a coalition with one or more parties to acquire a minimum of sixty-one seats. Disgruntled opposition MPs walked out of the parliament in protest (Letsie 2013: 65–67).

By ignoring the Coalition of Concerned Citizens' demands and undermining the democratic functions and processes of the parliament, the Prime Minister had turned himself into an enemy of the people. In the election, the Democratic Congress won forty-one out of eighty constituencies and received seven additional seats through Propositional Representation. The All-Basotho Convention, the major opposition party, won twenty-six seats (see Thabane 2017), and formed a coalition together with the Congress for Democracy and the National Party to make up the required two-thirds of the National Assembly. Thomas Thabane became the Prime Minister of Lesotho. This regime change gave people hope for change as they celebrated the overthrow of Pakalitha Mosisili's Congress government.

Mosisili's removal was significant in Lesotho's political history. The 'Congress–National' rhetoric and dichotomy finally came to an end. The National Party had been established in 1957 as a breakaway party from the Congress Party, which in turn had launched in 1952 as a national branch of the African Congress Party in South Africa (see Chapter 5).

Tensions between the two parties escalated after independence, leading to the exile of many influential leaders and members of the Congress Party who were only to return in the late 1980s in preparations for the 1993 elections. Throughout this time, people had to choose sides and politicians used this history of conflicts between the two to sway public opinion and amass popular support.

In 2012, neither the 'Nationals' nor 'Congress' could form a government on their own. After the 1986 coup, the National Party on the one hand had lost much of its legitimacy and support. Owing to its authoritarianism and elitism, the Congress Party on the other disintegrated from 1993, producing multiple offspring. The major opposition party at the time, the All-Basotho Convention, became the people's only viable option; however, it too could not command a majority. As a result, the country was subjected to a series of unstable coalition governments from 2012. In the five years following 2012, Lesotho held three snap elections, amid widespread violence, political instability, mismanagement of national resources and economic stagnation. Between 2012 and 2015, three parties formed government; seven between 2015 and 2017; and four since then (Thabane 2017). Mothibe (2017: 70–71) tells us that:

> The ABC-led coalition was a marriage of convenience which was driven by an 'anti-Mosisili sentiment' ... It was hoped that the political elite had, at last, come to their senses and were then committed to an inclusive nation-building process and economic development ... Alas, that was never to be, as political instability became more pronounced than ever before in the political history of the country because political elites vied for power at the expense of the people and embarked on bitter and most bloody struggle to get to the top.

Soon after occupying the position of Prime Minister, Thabane aggressively launched a massive anti-corruption campaign targeted at various key figures in the opposition, business, government and security forces. This ignited a spree of conflicts and killings as the latter worked to oust Thabane in retaliation. In June 2014, the estranged Prime Minister prorogued the parliament to subvert a vote of no confidence against him. Now determined to attain their objectives – by all means – Thabane's antagonists attempted a coup to overthrow him in August 2014. With close associates, they fled to South Africa (Mothibe 2017: 70–71).

In 2015, Lesotho went to elections in the absence of Thabane. Now led by the Democratic Congress, a new multiparty government was formed by seven parties. To cater for and reward those that assisted in the overthrow of Thabane, Prime Minister Pakathita Mosisili increased the cabinet from thirteen to twenty-three. Despite these changes, conflicts within the elites persisted leading to the death of Lieutenant-General Maaparankoe Mahao, the military commander. Thereafter, the Southern African Development Community (SADC) intervened setting up a commission of inquiry. Among others, the regional organisation recommended that Lesotho must hold elections in the presence of exiled leaders. In 2017 Thabane regained the position of Prime Minister after his party formed a coalition with three other parties.

Basotho were optimistic that Thabane would ensure peace and stability to foster development and address various socio-economic predicaments. The Prime Minister, however, turned against this mission. Several indicators highlighted his digressions. He stalled the implementation of SADC's security reforms. Like those before him, his government became authoritarian and mismanaged national resources. His young wife, Maesaiah Thabane, was central in Thabane's changed direction. The First Lady dictatorially meddled in party and government affairs, causing a division in the former and instigating the dismissal of some cabinet members (Burke 2020). In May 2020 the ruling party and opposition finally succeeded in forcing Thabane to resign.

Summary

In the context of elitism and authoritarian multiparty politics, we have seen in this chapter the rise of Basotho solidarity. The historical role played by the Basotho in national politics was amplified. This temporary success, however, was replaced by continuing political corruption and popular disaffection. The neocolonial character of Lesotho's rulers remained intact, and they continued to serve exclusive interests while sacrificing the people. Ironically, the elites also became suicidal, as violence continued mostly within their own circles.

The bravery of the Basotho, normally hidden, revealed itself in flashes, but this was not enough to dismantle a deeply rooted system of oppression. Through the 'Mother of All Protests' march, the people demanded that the Congress be reconciled with its own historic mission. They called for the reformation of the internal workings of our democracy in favour of the people and collective interests, and they clearly articulated the ruinous impact of market fundamentalism and patronage politics.

Despite their anger, they did not call for the expulsion of outsiders. Instead, they challenged Lesotho's government to allow the movement of people across borders. They insisted that the government renew the agenda of the 'Conquered Territories' with South Africa (see Chapter 2). In this way, they saw their fortunes as being permanently tied to the wider region, and to South Africa in particular.

NOTES

1. Interview with Simon Kuena Phafane, businessman, immediate former president of the Lesotho Chamber of Commerce and Industry, former Principle Secretary in the Ministry of Trade and Industry and Chief Executive Officer of the Basotho Enterprises Development Corporation, Maseru, September 2013; Minutes of the Meeting between the Principle Secretary of the Ministry of Trade and Industry with the Lesotho Chamber of Commerce and Industry, LCCI Head Office, Maseru, 19 March 2013.
2. Interview with Ntaote Seboka, Mosotho businessman and President of the Lesotho Chamber of Commerce and Industry, Maseru, August 2013; interview with Fako Hakane, Secretary General of the Lesotho Chamber of Commerce and Industry, Maseru, August 2013.
3. Interview with Phafane, September 2013; Minutes of the Meeting between the Principle Secretary of the Ministry of Trade and Industry with the Lesotho Chamber of Commerce and Industry, LCCI Head Office, Maseru, 19 March 2013.
4. Interview with ’Mammako Molapo, businesswoman, Founding Member of the Lesotho Liquor and Restaurant Owners Association and former Executive Member of the Lesotho Chamber of Commerce and Industry, Maseru, October 2013.
5. ‘Mosisili Rebuffs LCCI Demand on Funding’. Retrieved 15 August 2020 from lestimes.com/Mosisili-rebuffs-lcci-demand-on-funding.
6. Interview with Thuso Green, December 2014.
7. Interview with Thuso Green, December 2014.
8. Ibid.
9. Interview with Thabo Qhesi, Chief Executive Officer of the Private Sector Foundation of Lesotho, Maseru, September 2013.
10. Interview with Hakane, Maseru, August 2013; interview with Phafane, Maseru, September 2013; interview with Seboka, Maseru, August 2013.
11. ‘Mosisili Rebuffs LCCI Demand on Funding’. Retrieved 15 August 2020 from lestimes.com/Mosisili-rebuffs-lcci-demand-on-funding.
12. Interview with Tsietsi Chabatsane, Chairman of the Leribe Forestry Association and Leribe Chamber of Commerce and Industry, Leribe, December 2013.
13. Interview with Alicia Motšoane, businesswoman and President and Founding Member of Mafeteng Chamber of Business, Mafeteng, October 2013; interview with Bitsang Theoane, businesswoman and Founding Member of the Mafeteng Chamber of Business, October 2013.
14. ‘LRA Business Partnership Forum Launched’. Retrieved on 19 August 2020 from http://lestimes.com/lra-business-partnership-forum-launched/.
15. Interview with Phafane, Maseru, September 2013.
16. Interview with Lehlohonolo Chefa, Former President of the Junior Chamber International and Founding Member of the Consumer Protection Association, Maseru, November 2013.

17. 'COLETU protests reduced student intake at NUL'. Retrieved14 February 2019 from http://lestimes.com/coletu-protests-reduced-student-intake-at-nul/.
18. Ibid.
19. 'Police Foil Massive Protest March'. Retrieved on 15 February 2015 from http://lestimes.com/police-foil-massive-protest-march/.
20. Ibid.
21. Ibid.
22. Ibid.
23. Interview with 'Malitlou Morojele, businesswoman and former Chairperson of the Maseru Chamber of Commerce and Industry, October 2013.

REFERENCES

Burke, J. 2020. 'Lesotho PM Requests Immunity from Charge of Murdering Wife', *The Guardian*, 24 February. Retrieved 04 March 2020 from https://www.theguardian.com/world/2020/feb/24/lesotho-pm-thomas-thabane-surprise-court-appearance-over-wife-murder.

United States Federal Government. 2010. *Country Reports on Human Rights Practices for 2008 Volume I submitted for the Committee of Foreign Relations US Senate and Committee on Foreign Affairs US House of Representatives.* Washington: United States Government Printing Office.

Hart, K., J. Laville and A.D. Cattani. 2010. 'Building the Human Economy Together', in K. Hart, J. Laville and A.D. Cattani (eds), *The Human Economy: A Citizen's Guide.* Cambridge: Polity Press, pp. 1–17.

International Labour Organisation. 2012. 'Lesotho 2012 Baseline Report: Worker Perspectives from the Factory and Beyond'. Retrieved 14 February 2019 from https://www.google.com/amp/s/pdfslide.net/amp/documents/lesotho-baseline-report-better-work-baseline-report-worker-perspective-when.html.

'Lesotho: Nation's Mother of All Protests'. 2011. *AllAfrica*, 23 November 2011. Retrieved 28 February 2015 from http://allafrica.com/stories/201108230123.html.

'Lesotho Unions Merge'. 2015. *IndustriAll*, 3 June 2015. Retrieved 14 February 2019 from http://www.industriall-union.org/lesotho-unions-merge.

Letsie, T.W. 2013. 'The 2012 General Elections in Lesotho: A Step Towards the Consolidation of Democracy', *Journal of African Elections* 12(1): 65–83.

Manoeli, S. 2012. *Lesotho After AGOA: From Textile Boom to Sustainable Development: Discussion Paper 6/2012.* Johannesburg: The Brenthurst Foundation.

Ministry of Finance and Development Planning. 2004. *Lesotho Vision 2020: Empowerment for Prosperity.* Morija: Morija Printing Works.

Mothibe, T. 2017. 'Political Leadership Challenge in Lesotho – A Cause of Political Instability', in M. Thabane (ed.), *Towards an Anatomy of Persistent Political Instability in Lesotho, 1966–2016*. Roma: National University of Lesotho, pp. 47–73.

Sejanamane, M. 2017. *Struggle Against Impunity in Lesotho.* Morija: Morija Printers.

Setšabi, S., and R.C. Leduka. 2008. 'The Politics of Street Trading in Maseru', *Urban Forum* 19(3): 221–41.

Shakya, M. 2011. 'Apparel Exports in Lesotho: The State's Role in Building Critical Mass for Competitiveness', in P. Chuhan-Pole and M. Angwafo (eds), *Yes, Africa Can: Success Stories from a Dynamic Continent*. Washington DC: World Bank Publications, pp. 219–29.

Thabane, M. (ed.). 2017. *Towards an Anatomy of Persistent Political Instability in Lesotho, 1966–2016*. Roma: National University of Lesotho.

Tlali, C. 2012. 'Private Sector Foundation Investigates Members'. Retrieved on 19 August 2020 from http://sundayexpress.co.ls/private-sector-foundation-investigates-members/.

CHAPTER 9

The Rise of a Chinese Trading Monopoly and of Mobile Money, 2000s–2020

Introduction

By the 2000s, job opportunities in South African mines had shrunk for many young Basotho. As shown in the Introduction, Lesotho gained national independence when the South African mining industry began to decline. The country soon lost its historical position as a principal supplier of male labour to the mines. In the 1970s, there were approximately 130,000 Basotho employed in the mines, but the number had declined to 50,000 by the 1980s. More Basotho were retrenched from the 1990s onwards, and by 2011, there were only about 40,000 employed in South Africa as a whole (Central Bank of Lesotho 2011: 18).

South Africa became more inward-looking after the mid-1990s. When apartheid ended in 1994, the government introduced a new national identity (ID) system for all its citizens. Before, Africans were issued 'passbooks' (*dompas*, or 'dumb pass') that allowed them to reside in specific areas of the country – the 'townships' and 'Bantustans' (or homelands). They had to carry these everywhere they went.[1] The new ID system became the primary basis for resource allocation as the country aimed to address the poor living conditions of its own people. Many Basotho acquired South African citizenship and stayed. Others went home, but continued to move between the two countries as informal workers, traders and artisanal diamond diggers in closed mining shafts. In many ways, the Basotho and their home country were victims of this new regional reconfiguration.

This chapter shows that contrary to their hopes of returning to their 'home economy', Basotho faced a difficult reality – the rise of a Chinese trading monopoly. Many Basotho reinvested their gratuities in commerce, small-scale farming, poultry, informal small-scale real estate (*malaene*) and transport ('*combis*' and '4+1s'). A majority, with little capital, operated informal enterprises and ventured into artisanal diamond mining, wool and mohair production, livestock trading and handicrafts (Hoag 2018; Makhetha 2017; Polasi, Majara, Mohapi and Mosola 2015; Polasi, Mohapi and Majara 2015).

In 2008, there were an estimated 100,000 enterprises, employing about 300,000 Basotho (Government of Lesotho 2008: 1–2). Between 2013 and 2014, the Lesotho Bureau of Statistics conducted a census of formal businesses. Its report of May 2015 revealed that there were some 9,500 registered businesses around the country: 82 per cent were sole proprietors, concentrated in Maseru (26 per cent), with Leribe second (20 per cent) and Thaba-Tseka, in the mountain areas, lowest (4 per cent). Of these, about 600 were owned by foreign investors. Wholesale and retail (at 65 per cent) accounted for the largest share: over 6,000 registered businesses, many of them controlled by Chinese traders. Accommodation (mainly hotels and guest houses) followed at 12 per cent, while manufacturing came in third at about 10 per cent (Lesotho Bureau of Statistics 2015: vi–viii).

More than half of Lesotho's two million people now live below the poverty line, and a third fall below the extreme poverty line. From 2002 to 2017, national poverty remained around 60 per cent, and Lesotho ranked second highest for HIV/AIDS in Africa (Santho 2017: 117–23). From 23 per cent in 2008, unemployment increased to 32 per cent in 2012; in those years, it grew from 29 per cent to 38 per cent in urban areas, and from 20 per cent to 31 per cent in rural areas. It escalated from 26 per cent to 37 per cent among the youth (those aged 18–35) (Country Meters 2019).

This chapter examines the origins, activities and impact of Chinese traders in Lesotho. I highlight the Basotho's plural responses, in the context of the emergence of mobile money. This chapter thus reflects new aspects of Lesotho's economy. I locate these contemporary developments within the broader economic history of Lesotho. This period must be seen in the light of earlier periods, as the emergence of digital technologies in commerce potentially has something in common with the formative years of the early nineteenth century. We saw in Chapter 1 that the Basotho used technology, money and markets to shape their future. The current Basotho generation can learn from this earlier history while building their own economic future in the context of these new competing global forces.

Arrival of the Chinese Traders

In 2006, China passed the 'Africa Policy Paper', outlining its strategic and long-term development commitment to the African continent. Since then, China's involvement in Africa has generated fierce debates among scholars, development experts and policymakers. Discussion of China–Africa relations bifurcates between what we may call 'protagonists' and 'anatomists'. Generally, the latter see the Chinese in Africa as 'new colonialists' with predatory and imperial purposes. The former view them conversely as partners in a hierarchal but 'win-win' form of co-operation – in sharp contrast to the nineteenth and twentieth-century relations between Europe and Africa (Cheru and Obi 2010; Konings 2007; Lumumba-Kasongo 2007).

Key forums such as the China–Africa Forum, Asia–Africa Summit and Forum on China–Africa Cooperation (FOCAC), as well as China's influential role as one of the BRICs (Brazil, Russia, India, China and South Africa), have consolidated China's economic grip on Africa. Since the 'Africa Policy Paper', China has increased its investment, trade and aid ties, while working tirelessly to secure energy and mineral resources from the continent. In this way, China jumped on the bandwagon of neoliberal globalisation that followed the Washington Consensus (Cheru and Obi 2010: 1–9).

As happened in many African states, the Congress government in Lesotho turned to the East and strengthened its Sino–African relations. China readily pumped money into the economy, building roads, schools and libraries, and supporting politicians (Ntsukunyane 2019). China even went so far as to construct a new parliament building. From the mid-2000s, 'China' was a buzzword in Lesotho's political, bureaucratic and economic corridors. Political and business elites flew regularly to China to strike deals and attract investors in the name of South–South co-operation. The government's relations with China opened the economy to East Asian traders, all of whom are called 'Chinese' by Basotho. These traders arrived in large numbers from the late 1990s and early 2000s, and soon came to dominate local commerce, replacing European traders.

China did not build its relations with Africa from scratch; it strengthened and expanded ties of some standing. Beyond bilateral state relations, these ties were facilitated by corporations and transnational mobility anchored on kinship economic networks. Lesotho has its own history with China beyond the formal contemporary Sino–Africa partnership. The emergent Chinese traders' monopoly of the local economy is connected to this history of human mobility across national borders.

Before 1973, the colonial government had restricted Indian traders to operating in selected parts of the country, to lessen their competition with European traders. The National Party government passed a Trade Ordinance of 1973 to free the country's local businesses, since Lesotho was now following the capitalist path. This law lifted the restriction on Indian traders' areas of operation. These Indian traders had strong trading links with South Africa (Natal) and India; with free local mobility, they were able to expand their business activities across the country's major business centres. Their impact on local trade did not last long, however. Around the millennium, waves of Fujianese arrived, building on kinship and economic networks created by Taiwanese and Shanghainese business communities before.

After independence, Lesotho had established relations with several countries and international organisations to secure development aid and industrial investment. Taiwan was one of these countries. As part of its development assistance mission, the Taiwanese government sent skilled teams to Lesotho, mostly in medicine and agriculture. Upon completion of their mission, several remained to pursue opportunities in local commerce (Turner 2014: 40).

In addition to these experts, more Taiwanese arrived after 1974, as investors and administrators in Lesotho's export-led textile and garments industries (ibid.: 40–42). Their transnational mobility was enabled by the Multi-Fibre Agreement (1974–2005), which introduced quotas for textiles and garments on developing countries' exports to United States and European markets. Several developing countries, including Lesotho, were exempted from the Agreement; as a result, it was easier for the Taiwanese to transfer their business interests to these countries. Lesotho thus became a favourable destination for investment (Turner 2014; Shakya 2011; Manoeli 2012).

The flows of skilled Taiwanese employees declined in the early 1990s as they responded to more lucrative job opportunities in mainland China. Factory owners recruited cheaper skilled labour from the mainland, as they were reluctant to employ local Basotho in such high positions. The first groups to seize these employment opportunities were skilled workers from Shanghai, recruited through private labour agencies. Like the Taiwanese, some of these Shanghainese migrants took advantage of opportunities in Lesotho's local business. They opened clothing outlets, building and construction hardware businesses, motor-vehicle spare-parts shops, and groceries and manufactured-goods stores. They sold items imported either directly from China and Taiwan or through South Africa-based suppliers, mostly in Johannesburg and Durban (Turner 2014: 43–44).

By the late 1990s, it had become difficult for Taiwanese factory owners in Lesotho to recruit skilled cheap labour from Shanghai. This was due to increased economic growth in the coastal regions of China, which attracted skilled local labour. Consequently, factory owners sought other avenues to find cheap labour. The province of Fujian provided them with such an alternative, but the Fujianese were not highly skilled workers (Turner 2014: 50). Many of them entered local commerce. From 1998, the influx of young-to-middle-aged Fujianese migrants increased. Their mobility from China to Lesotho via Johannesburg was facilitated by human-traffickers known as 'snakeheads', who are paid to organise their visas and boarding passes (ibid.: 52–55).

Economic Networks in the Rise of a Chinese Trading Monopoly

The Fujianese flock into Lesotho because they believe that there is 'easy money' to be made there (Turner 2014: 52–55). They organise themselves into informal networks connected to two local Chinese Associations: Fuqing Association and the Association of Chinese Enterprises. New arrivals are lent money to join established informal arrangements for collective bulk-buying and transportation. This allows them to sell at lower prices and reduce transport costs across the country (ibid.).

With their access to capital and ability to cut prices, the Fujianese can drive out Basotho traders, whose financial muscle is weak. In this way, Fujianese traders have quickly become hegemonic. They employ some locals initially, to discover the numbers and status of relevant local Basotho businesses; with this information, they open businesses and lower their prices on key items. When local competitors look unstable, they offer to buy their businesses. Locals can hardly refuse. Turner suggests that:

> The profitability of the periphery is ensured by a centrifugal force that pushes new arrivals away from areas where a strong Fujianese presence already exists ... This is because the Fujianese model relies on total monopoly over tiny village markets. The Fujianese specialise in driving out local competitors and establishing small regimes of hegemony... [The system ensures that the] prices at which these goods are sold are always calculated to be cheaper than the local competitor... [Importantly,] specific businesses are targeted as rivals and Fujianese traders, supported by capital borrowed from a local Chinese association, will operate at a loss until the local competitor has been driven out of the market... Success is virtually guaranteed ... As soon as the local competitor looks shaky, the Fujianese will send a representative to negotiate the purchase of the failing shop'. (Turner 2014: 60–64)

A local Mosotho businesswoman in the central highlands corroborated: 'Competition from the Chinese traders is quite strong. We have tried to outsmart them, but they come to us to investigate how we conduct our small businesses'.[2]

This hegemonic economic strategy is also fostered by the Fujianese's economic responsibilities. They are entangled in a complex web of money: they must repay loans secured from the associations, which are typically issued at high interest rates. They must share the costs of transport and other costs of operating business in remote areas of the country, and make remittances to families back home. These factors have forced them to operate on slim profit margins, in remote mountain regions and under difficult conditions. They live on their business premises to cut expenses, and avoid incurring costs by keeping their money with them, instead of depositing it in local banks They are also often accused of tax evasion.[3]

Basotho Outcry

The Chinese traders' displacement of Basotho traders, with the lenient support of the Congress government, created a backlash of public outcry, protests and xenophobia among various segments of the population. Anti-Asian sentiment among Basotho dates to the colonial period, when Indian traders arrived in the country. Apart from the 'Manthabiseng episode discussed in the Introduction, however, violent responses towards the Asians have been rare.

Other than this violent episode, Basotho reactions have typically taken the form of complaints against 'an influx of Chinese immigrants that come to Lesotho under the pretext of being skilled workers [and now] conquer the territory of small traders throughout the country' (*Public Eye*, 20–27 January 2006: 3). Parliamentarian M. Tšuluba of the Qoaling constituency in Maseru said:

> Basotho businesses … are now facing serious problems which are caused amongst others, by unfair competition from foreigners (the Fujianese) engaged in small businesses who use fraudulent methods to account for their tax obligations, a practice which makes them pay no taxes and empowers them to under-sell Basotho businesses.[4]

In addition, there have been complaints by Basotho that some Chinese traders have extended their business activities into the informal economy, through employing local Basotho to sell fruits, vegetables, mobile airtime and clothes on the streets. M.F. Mothae, a Member of Parliament, complained as early as 2002 that the Chinese migrants 'sell their goods on the streets thereby competing with street vendors'.[5] One Mosotho businesswoman in the district of Mafeteng added: 'What I hate the most, and see the Chinese do, is that they buy a lot of stock', and because they are financially stronger, 'they pay young [Basotho] boys to sell their things such as apples on the streets as hawkers'.[6]

Furthermore, the Fujianese traders have been heavily criticised for selling poor-quality equipment and spoiled foodstuffs. Because of their bulk-buying arrangements, they are forced to store food for longer periods, and to sell items beyond their expiry date. Long-established Taiwanese have also expressed their dissatisfaction with Fujianese business practices, since the Basotho see all East Asians as the 'Chinese'. Taiwanese feel that 'their good reputation in Lesotho ha[s] been tarnished by the unscrupulous practices of recent Fujianese migrants' (Turner 2014: 67).

Despite heated political reactions, local Basotho consumers continue to rely on Chinese traders' markets and affordable goods. The Chinese break bulk products and repackage some items, such as teabags, sugar and mealie-meal, into smaller affordable packages (ibid.: 68). Three out of five Chinese premises are rented from Indians, and the other two from Basotho (McNamee 2012: 28), while many Basotho supply the Chinese with a variety of locally produced commodities and import cheaper manufactured goods from China.

Invoking History: The Re-emergence of 'Thekommoho'

It was June 2013. The sun was slowly melting the morning's winter frost as I approached a group of about seventy Basotho, holding a meeting in a warehouse located in the premises of the Basotho Enterprises Development Corporation (BEDCO) in Maseru (see Chapter 7). I was to meet a potential informant taking part in the meeting. I tiptoed cautiously at the margins of the gathering, with the aim of not causing any disruptions or drawing attention to myself. I approached a man to confirm if I was at the right place. Yes, I was told, but my interviewee had urgently left after a phone call.

I had arrived close to the end of the meeting, as the chair was giving his closing remarks – really more a reaffirmation of solidarity. 'It's our only refuge. We must work hard. Let's continue to buy together otherwise the Chinese will take over and we will be left with nothing'. I turned my head towards the applauding crowd as the chairman concluded. In a disorderly fashion, the group took off to a far corner of the warehouse. I asked the gentleman who was my companion again: 'What's going on?' He paused. 'We buy together. This is Theko 'Moho', he said, as I allowed him to join the others.

Written differently, the name of this co-operative (Theko 'Moho) is the same as that of the 1960s Thekommoho bulk-buying co-operative (see Chapter 7). As with the previous organisation, annual membership fees covered operational costs. Logistics were facilitated by elected committees organised around the chairperson, their vice-chairperson, the secretary general, their deputy, the treasurer and two committee members (often respected individuals that were not necessarily active, but advised the group).

Not only did the co-operatives share a name and structure, they were formed with similar principles and motives. They were meant to pool resources to 'buy together' and counter foreign traders' dominance and marginalisation of the Basotho. The new Theko 'Moho was formed when many Basotho were feeling pressure from the Chinese traders. Through the co-operative, members contributed money into a common pool with which to buy from local and South African wholesalers and producers in bulk and then share proportionally (*Lesotho Business*, January 13–19, 2010: 9, translated from Sesotho).[7]

Members of the co-operative focused on staple foods and those commodities that were difficult for shop owners to acquire individually. They selected priority items to buy on a weekly basis, with priority given to necessities like milk, bread, eggs and others. A member of the co-operative, Mosito Chopo, affirmed: 'Honestly, Theko 'Moho is very strong. It is strong because right now, we are not able to fight the Chinese individually – when you go to the wholesale alone you are given [stock] at a high price'. After members came together, Chopo said that they 'we are given [stock] at the same price as the Chinese'.[8]

The co-operative grew in popularity and efficiency. For some time, it was a model of a political and pragmatic way forward for the Basotho, nostalgically built on history. In January 2010, *Lesotho Business*, a local newspaper, reported: 'This association of theirs has helped a lot of [Basotho] business owners since their businesses were collapsing … It has helped them [to] compete with foreigners' (13–19 January 2010: 9). Due to internal conflicts and financial difficulties, however, the co-operative's efficiency dwindled. Like many small organisations (see Chapter 8), it was moribund by the late 2010s.

Development of Mobile Money

Mobile money in Basotho-owned businesses developed in the context of the rise of the Chinese traders' monopoly. Basotho businesses are now part of the new financial ecosystem that brings together big and small actors. Controlled by the mobile phone network operators, the Basotho are agents who facilitate the movement of money across the country and its borders. In 1996, Vodacom launched its operations in Lesotho, and Econet Telecom arrived in 2008. Due to their activities, Lesotho's teledensity – the number of people using mobile phones per hundred inhabitants – increased from 1 per cent in 2002 to 84 per cent in 2013. By 2014, Vodacom was the leading mobile phone operator, with an estimated one million subscribers and a market share of some 80 per cent (Lesotho Communications Authority 2014).

Econet and Vodacom respectively introduced mobile money in 2012 ('Eco-cash') and 2013 ('M-Pesa'). Designed as a mobile-based non-bank financial product, mobile money was first developed in Kenya in 2007 by Safaricom, a subsidiary of Vodacom. It was launched as a grassroots mobile phone-based system for transfers of small amounts of money, through person-to-person transfers and involving largely unbanked and under-banked people. 'M' stands for 'mobile' and '*pesa*' means 'money' in Swahili (Agar 2013).

In 2012, the First National Bank (FNB) of South Africa introduced its mobile-banking product, FNB 'e-Wallet', with the aim of serving unbanked communities. The FNB 'e-Wallet' allows holders to send money to any mobile phone number, whether or not they have a bank account (Coupienne and Soglonou 2013: 21). The FNB is one of Lesotho's four banks, along with Standard Bank, Nedbank (both also based in South Africa) and Post Bank (fully state-owned). Apart from these, there are insurance companies, non-bank financial microlenders and co-operatives which make money transfers (ibid.: 10).

Between 2012 and 2017, mobile phones transformed local business and the financial economy in Lesotho. Many Basotho businesses now show mobile-money placards. People no longer depend on bus drivers, friends, family, colleagues and acquaintances to deliver 'parcels' (*phasele*, or money). About 75 per cent of Lesotho's population lives in the rural mountains, which have poor amenities and infrastructure. The banking system is in some ways as restrictive as South Africa's, to which it is tied. Most people are not banked; only 7 per cent of adults have access to credit from commercial banks (FinMark Trust 2011). A report by FinMark Trust (ibid.: 14) established that 37 per cent of income in the rural areas comes from farming, 9 per cent from wages, 12.5 per cent from private pensions, 10 per cent from enterprises, 12 per cent from family and friends, 10 per cent from government pensions and 7 per cent from other government welfare grants.

Mobile money assumed wider relevance and applicability from around 2015, when it became a mobile-based payments system through which people could pay utility bills (water and electricity), pay school fees, receive social grants, renew digital satellite-television subscriptions, purchase airtime and much more. From being a payment system, it also evolved into a mobile-based financial system. People started using it to save money, manage their finances and procure insurance, particularly life insurance. Mobile money is now indispensable to people's self-organised credit and savings schemes, or *stokvels* (Maliehe 2018).

In March 2013, the Central Bank of Lesotho observed that there had been an estimated 62-per-cent increase in the use of mobile money (Central Bank of Lesotho 2013: 4). The concentration of Basotho businesses across the country has an impact on the distribution of agents and delivery of mobile financial services: Maseru accounts for 39 per cent of all Lesotho agents, while all other districts have less than 10 per cent except for Mafeteng, which accounts for 11 per cent (ibid.: 19–20).

Summary

Following the collapse of the mining economy, local commerce was the Basotho's one hope of improvement. Many now have nowhere to go other than government employment, where most of the rewards stay at the top (see Chapter 7). First the Indians, and now the Chinese, have demonstrated better successes than the Basotho. The British disrupted Basotho trade by political means and greater capital (see Parts 1 and 2); with little capital, we have seen in this chapter that the Basotho are persistently vulnerable to powerful global forces.

In local politics, this has heightened a sense that, as always, the rulers never had people's interests at heart. In a changing economic landscape, reactions to this were diverse. Learning from their past, some Basotho revamped the co-operative movement, but with internal conflicts and little structural support, they could not reproduce earlier successes. We also saw in the previous chapter that they formed a solidarity movement in defence of their social fabric and out of a desperate need to cultivate a meaningful say and level of participation in the economic matters that affect their lives.

In the context of these hardships, mobile money gave Basotho a practical means to diversify their businesses. Despite a successful take-off, there are numerous challenges to overcome. For one, the exponential growth of mobile money strains Basotho agents, who lack adequate cash flows to meet increasing demands. As seen in the Introduction, the government and international organisations are investing in efforts to use mobile money to address the country's financial and economic hardships. On the ground, people are already shaping the use of these digital services.

The Basotho must learn from their own history. Technology and commerce influenced expansion in the nineteenth century. Though technology, money and markets have driven persistent inequality, Basotho history shows that they may help people build a better economic future. In this chapter, I have attempted to update readers on new developments in local commerce, while making the point that there are historical antecedents for what is currently emerging.

NOTES

1. The *dompass* was one of the most protested symbols of the apartheid system.
2. Interview with 'Maseala Seala, businesswoman, Thaba-Tseka, January 2014.
3. Parliamentary Debates (*Hansard*), First Meeting, Sixth Session, 12 August 2002, 4.
4. Ibid.
5. Parliamentary Debates (*Hansard*), Third Meeting, Fifth Session, 8 February 2002, 1.
6. Interview with 'Manthabiseng Mpitso, Mosotho businesswoman, Mafeteng, October 2013.
7. Interview with Mosito Chopo and Tlokotsi Letsie, businessmen and Members of Theko 'Moho, Maseru, October 2013.
8. Ibid.

REFERENCES

Agar, J. [2003] 2013. *Constant Touch: A Global History of the Mobile Phone.* London: Icon Books Ltd.

Central Bank of Lesotho. 2011. *Central Bank of Lesotho Quarterly Report – 2011.* Retrieved 15 April 2018 from https://www.centralbank.org.ls/images/Publications/Research/Reports/QuarterlyReviews/2011/Quart_Review_Jun_2011.pdf.

———. 2013. *Central Bank of Lesotho Annual Report – 2013.* Retrieved 20 July 2016 from https://www.centralbank.org.ls/images/Publications/Research/Reports/Annual/ANNUAL-REPORT-2013.pdf.

Cheru, F., and C. Obi (eds). 2010. *The Rise of China and India in Africa: Challenges, Opportunities and Critical Perspectives.* New York: Zed Books.

Coupienne, F., and M. Soglonou. 2013. Mobile Money for the Poor: Lesotho Scoping Report. Unpublished Commissioned Study Report by the United Nations Capital Development Fund, January–February.

FinMark Trust. 2011. *FinMark Trust's FinScope Lesotho: Top Line Findings Report – 2011*. Retrieved 15 April 2018 from https://finmark.org.za/finscope-lesotho-2011/.

Government of Lesotho. 2008. *The State of Small Enterprises in Lesotho*. Maseru: Lesotho Government Printers.

Hoag, C. 2018. 'The Ovicaprine Mystique: Livestock Commodification in Postindustrial Lesotho', *American Anthropology* 120(4): 725–37.

Konings, P. 2007. 'China and Africa in the Era of Neo-liberal Globalization', *CODESRIA Bulletin* 1 & 2: 17–22.

Lesotho Bureau of Statistics. 2015. *2013/2014 Economic Activity Census: Business Register Volume I*. Maseru: Lesotho Government Printers.

Lesotho Communications Authority. 2014. *Annual Report 2014*. Retrieved 20 July 2016 from www.lca.org.ls.

'Lesotho Population'. 2020. *Worldometer*. Retrieved 10 August 2020 from http://www.worldometer.info/world-population/lesotho-population.

Lumumba-Kasongo, T. 2007. 'China–Africa Relations in the Post-Cold War Era', *CODESRIA Bulletin* 1 & 2: 8–16.

Makhetha, E.L. 2017. 'Small Scale Artisanal Diamond Mining and Rural Livelihood Diversification in Lesotho', Ph.D. dissertation. Pretoria: University of Pretoria.

Maliehe, S. 2018. 'Demand for Mobile Money among Rural and Low-Income Populations in Lesotho', commissioned research report prepared under the 'Scaling Inclusion through Mobile Money' (SIMM) project, United Nations Lesotho, Central Bank of Lesotho, FinMark Trust and Ministry of Finance, April 2018.

Manoeli, S. 2012. *Lesotho After AGOA: From Textile Boom to Sustainable Development: Discussion Paper 6/2012*. Johannesburg: The Brenthurst Foundation.

McNamee, T. 2012. *Africa in their Words: A Study of Chinese Traders in South Africa, Lesotho, Botswana, Zambia and Angola Discussion Paper 2012/03*. Johannesburg: The Brenthurst Foundation.

Ntsukunyane, L. 2018. 'Chinese Business Tycoon Reveals How He Helped Politicians in Lesotho – But Denies Claims of State Capture', *Daily Maverick*, 1 November 2018. Retrieved 16 December 2019 from https://www.dailymaverick.co.za/article/2018-11-01-chinese-business-tycoon-reveals-how-he-helped-fund-politicians-in-lesotho-but-denies-claim-of-state-capture/.

Polasi, S., M. Majara, M. Mohapi and M. Mosola. 2015. 'Barriers to Development and Progress of Entrepreneurs: Case of Lesotho', *International Journal of Recent Research in Interdisciplinary Sciences* 2(3): 10–16.

Polasi, S., M. Mohapi and M. Majara. 2015. 'Socio-Economic Status of Women in Lesotho', *International Journal of Recent Research in Interdisciplinary Sciences* 2(3): 55–61.

Santo, S. 2017. 'Can Lesotho Survive? The Political Economy of a Fragile State', in M. Thabane (ed.), *Towards an Anatomy of Persistent Political Instability in Lesotho, 1966–2016*. Roma: National University of Lesotho, pp. 75–100.

Shakya, M. 2011. 'Apparel Exports in Lesotho: The State's Role in Building Critical Mass for Competitiveness', in P. Chuhan-Pole and M. Angwafo (eds), *Yes, Africa Can: Success Stories from a Dynamic Continent.* Washington DC: World Bank Publications, pp. 219–29.

Turner, M. 2014. 'Rethinking the Peripheral: Chinese Migrants in Lesotho', M.A. dissertation. Oxford: University of Oxford.

Conclusion

Commerce as Politics

Using archival material, oral histories, published sources and ethnographic insights, this book has compared three major phases of Lesotho's economic history from the early nineteenth century onwards. These were: the precolonial period (1820s–70s), the colonial period (1870s–1960s) and the postcolonial period (1966–2020). In conclusion, I will summarise and discuss key lessons illuminated by these phases, seen through the link between commerce and politics. My main focus has been on how the Basotho shaped their economy despite the odds stacked obstinately against them. Their self-determination, plural economic pragmatism, desire for economic advancement, alliance-making abilities and willingness to confront their rulers are palpable features of this history.

This study has been framed by a human economy approach. In a global context of competing interests, such an approach puts local people at the centre. A human economy is not handed down to the people, nor is it merely a reflection of what they are doing on the ground. It brings together small-scale humanism and large impersonal institutions. What people *do* is intricately connected to the big, impersonal world beyond their immediate reach. Those who use a human economy approach choose to learn from what people do, not just by themselves, but in pragmatic partnerships with bureaucracies, institutions and corporations that support their democratic interests. Money, markets and technology are indispensable to a human economy (Hart et al. 2010; Hart and Sharp 2014; Hart 2015, 2017).

This book synthesises how commerce and politics make and remake each other across the three phases. In Lesotho, commerce is a locus of political expression, and its actors play a significant role in politics and governance. Across time and space, Basotho have used money and markets to emancipate themselves from repressive rulers and institutions. Commerce facilitates a democratic aspiration for inclusion and social extension: Basotho have persistently reached out to the world beyond their locality for economic advancement and political autonomy. This book has demonstrated that despite conditions of poverty, repression and violence, a two-century-long Basotho struggle for economic independence still continues.

The modern Basotho nation emerged after the Lifaqane/Mfecane upheavals of the early nineteenth century. The nation's rise under Moshoeshoe and his allies coincided with Evangelical anti-slavery crusades and a global economy after the Napoleonic Wars (1803–15), when the British took over the Cape from the Dutch. From the outset, the Basotho were influenced by the particular regional experience of this world history. Using new agricultural technologies introduced by Europeans – missionaries, Afrikaners and British – the Basotho positioned themselves to generate significant economic growth in the Southern African region by the mid-century. By the 1870s, Lesotho was the 'granary' of mining towns in South Africa.

Despite hierarchies based on racial, religious and identity differences, the Basotho formed alliances founded on common interests, within and outside their territory. Mutuality and reciprocity enforced interdependence in pursuits of diverse ends. With protection from Moshoeshoe and support from the missionaries, various Basotho groups produced for local and distant markets. Others worked for the Europeans. These groups used money and markets to build their own wealth (comprising property, livestock and homes) while trying to emancipate themselves from an economy dominated by the chiefs.

The uncertainty and conflicts of the nineteenth century reinforced the legitimacy of the chiefs, who controlled wealth – land and livestock – and their use. Those who traded and worked in the Cape and the Free State introduced to the rest of the Basotho the transformative potential of horses and guns. In turn, these two instruments allowed the Basotho to maintain a degree of political autonomy under precarious conditions of war, land loss and starvation.

Commerce and technology offered a means of emancipation, inclusion and social extension, and political conditions cultivated by Moshoeshoe and the missionaries enabled plural individual rights to thrive. In these formative years, these factors shaped the collective social-democratic ethos and the advancement of the collective. Individuals shaped their world as much as it shaped them. Rooted in their localities, people could move in and out of their society, where economic production and social reproduction took place. The Basotho had abundant land to support their pursuits. Money and markets connected home to the regional economy, with free movement and limited restrictions.

The discovery and exploitation of minerals in South Africa in the late nineteenth century marked the beginning of a new epoch – the period of colonialism. This was a reversal of the previous regional economic formation, which was based on greater interdependence. From the 1870s, the British shifted from their protectionist approach when Moshoeshoe requested intervention against Afrikaner aggressions and land conquest. They now used political means and big capital to dismantle Basotho economic independence and to meet the increasing labour demands in the mines.

Working with the chiefs, they imposed colonial laws, a rigid bureaucratic system and stringent taxation regimes to extract labour. From then on, social mobility was directed mainly to the mines. Effectively, the people's survival depended on wages and subsistence agriculture. Furthermore, these new economic formations were based on coercion and disenfranchisement of the people. The Basotho lost a significant degree of freedom and independence, and the social cohesion of the earlier years had little room to mature. By the late nineteenth century, the missionaries themselves were worried about what they saw as the 'love of gain' among individual Basotho. Economic individualism was fast ruining the social fabric and religious ideals that had made the earlier successes possible, and the collectivist practices of *matsema* became less central as the chiefs profiteered from them.

Colonialism shaped Lesotho's economy as an enclave of cheap labour. As men left for the mines, commerce emerged as the main pillar of the local economy. Colonial reforms after the 1870s shifted trade from precolonial formations to rigidly regulated forms, and the new economy came to be dominated by European traders, who monopolised commerce. Through the Chamber of Commerce, they worked with the colonial administration to restrict the issuance of trading licences and other business opportunities to Basotho and Indians.

It was only after the mid-1950s, and a protracted struggle, that more Basotho broke into colonial commerce. The role of missionary-educated groups and mineworkers was instrumental in leading the Basotho anticolonial protests of the early twentieth century and fighting for the inclusion of Basotho in commerce. These groups introduced urban politics to the rural masses. Through their early organisations – the Progressive Association, the League of Commoners, the League of Justice and the Basuto Traders Association – the Basotho protested exclusion and sought to reform local commerce. As a result, politics in commerce became more confrontational.

The political activities of these organisations have been well documented in Lesotho historiography, but their activism in commerce has received little attention. As a result, little is known about the economic aspect of the liberation struggle, and more particularly about how these early organisations laid the foundations for the independence movement from the mid-1950s onwards. As a result of their efforts, movements towards self-determination sat alongside an aspiration to control commerce and undermine the Europeans' monopoly. The Basotho resisted incorporation into South Africa and vehemently fought for their sovereignty.

Lesotho finally attained national independence in 1966. The Basotho were optimistic that independence would produce conditions suitable for economic autonomy. As a result, they resuscitated their business association and formed a bulk-buying co-operative, Thekommoho. Their aim was to solve their long-standing problems of access to credit and supply of stock. Their subsequent success stemmed not only from self-organisation but also from how they redefined their relations with large South African companies. As they had done in precolonial times, they extended themselves as equal partners, based on mutual interests and exchange. Although they were in actuality not equals, they attempted to forge economic relations of interdependence based on trade, despite border restrictions. Relations were hierarchical and based on debt, trust and solidarity.

The efforts of Basotho traders were undermined both by the postcolonial government and by European traders. The two worked to protect each other's political and economic interests. Prime Minister Leabua Jonathan's National Party and his regime were supported by the chiefs and Europeans, particularly the Catholic Church and European traders. The latter considered the radical Pan-Africanist approach of the Congress Party as 'communist' in ideology, despite the existence of Communist Party of Lesotho as well. As an offspring of the African National Congress (ANC), the Congress Party was the vanguard of the liberation struggle in Lesotho.

The government and the Europeans used violence, money, political influence and legal apparatus to destroy Thekommoho. This colonial legacy laid fertile grounds for neocolonialism, which persisted thereafter: postcolonial governments added violence to the rigid administration developed by the colonial government for the extraction of labour, and ruling parties replicated the *comprador* role that the chiefs had previously held, serving foreign interests at the expense of their own people.

After 1970, the National Party ruled dictatorially. As is well documented in Lesotho, it used development intervention to advance despotism. I have demonstrated that the government used the same approach even in more urban-based spheres of the economy, such as commerce and big business. It used the mask of the developmental state model to control the economy. The state became so powerful that it seamlessly squashed the Congress uprising in 1974. Exiled politicians re-strategised abroad, while those who stayed behind were weakened and had little power to resist state intervention. The Lesotho Chamber of Commerce and Industry was born in 1976 under these conditions. With stronger regional and international Pan-Africanist networks, Basotho became a force within the Chamber; by the 1990s, they were controlling the institution, as more Europeans left the country.

The 1990s were a watershed moment in the country's contemporary history. First, in a context of increasing population, Lesotho lost its position as the main supplier of male labour to the South African mines. Second, the military toppled the civilian dictatorship of Leabua Jonathan in 1986 and subsequently adopted the IMF's market-economy policies. The resulting poverty and unemployment caused popular unrest, and people protested the military dictatorship and called for democracy. As seen in the 'Manthabiseng uprising, popular sentiments continued to hold that the government was supporting foreign investors, this time East Asians. Third, with mounting pressure from regional and international communities, exiled Congress Party leaders returned in the late 1980s in preparation for elections that finally took place in 1993.

If there was any hope for a Basotho revival, it was in local commerce. However, an influx of Chinese traders arrived in Lesotho in the context of neoliberal globalisation. Within a decade, they were in control of the economy and supporting local politicians. Reactions from Basotho were diverse: while xenophobia increased, some Basotho forged new economic alliances with the Chinese, while others turned to co-operatives that they organised themselves. After a few years, Thekommoho re-emerged as Basotho sought to address their financial problems and counter the Chinese traders' monopoly. However, economic hardship and political instability ensured that the Basotho's economic efforts could not produce lasting results.

When the Congress Party assumed power, they abandoned their historic mission to advance people's interests and continued with free-market policies, privatising state-owned companies. Through the enriching of the elites, the state became their thiefdom; various institutions and development programmes were used as means to build party fellowship and usurp taxes, customs revenues, development assistance and the proceeds of foreign investments. In response, Basotho traders took a leading role in mobilising the people, as they had done before. They were the first to experience economic exclusion and the impact of the Chinese traders' monopoly.

By the 2000s, the majority of Basotho were experiencing the ruinous impacts of market fundamentalism, elitism, patronage politics and corruption. It became increasingly difficult for graduates without political connections to secure jobs in government, non-governmental organisations and private companies. The quality of healthcare, education, infrastructure, and living and working conditions declined further.

In 2011, various associations and trade unions formed the 'Coalition of Concerned Citizens'. In August, they launched the country's biggest ever march ('The Mother of All Protests'), demanding that the government reform and democratise the economy. Basotho called for a more inclusive economy and for well-equipped bureaucracies that responded to the needs of the poor, not just to those with money and influence.

This solidarity movement played a crucial role in the collapse of the Congress regimes that had held power since 1993. It ended Prime Minister Mosisili's rule of a decade and half. In many respects, however, regime change was not followed by the desired results: Prime Minister Thabane, who had emerged as a popular source of hope, turned against his mission to serve the country and the people. The country was plunged into a series of unstable coalition governments characterised by corruption and violence. The ruling elites aggravated economic stagnation, and peripheralised development, democracy and the people's interests. As a result, the country continued to depend overly on SACU revenues, South Africa, development support and foreign investment.

During the 'Mother of All Protests', the Basotho issued a clarion call to the government to allow the free movement of people across the border and revive the agenda of 'Conquered Territories' in the Free State. The restoration of these territories may be impossible, but the Basotho recognised that their history and future are intricately intertwined with South Africa's. Negotiating a new arrangement with South Africa as part of an attempt to dismantle the current unequal and prejudicial relationship is central for Basotho economic struggles in the twenty-first century.

Confronting rulers in domestic politics and regime change is not the end of the struggle for self-determination. Self-sufficiency at home is connected to the world outside. Colonialism, and its antithesis in liberation, shaped national consciousness and created nation-state structures of economic dependency. The mission for the Basotho is to reconcile the contradictions of this formation and rediscover a relationship of greater equality with South Africa, despite inherent hierarchies.

The immediate post-Mfecane rise and expansion of the Basotho in the region contradicts the claims made by their colonial and postcolonial rulers that they lack resilience and initiative as agents in a modern political economy. When Thekommoho was established and Basotho took control of the Chamber of Commerce, their drive for economic independence was inseparable from their ability to forge relations with the outside world.

Rigid constructions of national identity work mostly for the rulers, not the majority who continue to struggle to break through forces confining their self-determination. Colonialism established these rigid confines in order to extract cheap labour, and neocolonialism then perpetuated that legacy. South Africa has played a massive role in exploiting regional economies such as that of Lesotho; the migrant-labour system and the 1986 border blockade, leading to the signing of the Highlands Water Treaty, are extreme examples of this. In various historical moments, we learn that the Basotho's powers of self-organisation point to future pathways of economic success and political autonomy.

Politicians in Lesotho use the rhetoric of common history – the history of the Basotho under Moshoeshoe and the Congress struggle – to legitimise their domination. This history is an 'opium' used to disguise their sinister economic and political motives. These politicians still use 'development' as an altruistic mask for disabling the people. Just like their colonial predecessors, they claim that Basotho lack modern business skills and enterprise.

Like other groups in this region, the Basotho have not attained an economy that is based even remotely on social justice; poverty, inequality and repression hold sway. The Basotho must revisit their history, and this book is one attempt at this. Through increased solidarity, the Basotho need to dismantle the 'survival of the fittest' individualism propagated by market policies. Through their early political and business organisations, Basotho used missionary education to fight colonialism and sought to reform colonial commerce without denying their own philosophy of solidarity. By the mid-1950s, there were more Basotho in commerce due to their pressure for inclusion. Based on cultural practices of collectivism, the Basotho also rekindled the co-operative spirit. This study provides solid grounds pointing to what they could achieve in the future.

Bleak as Lesotho's recent history may be, the successful development of mobile money in local commerce by Basotho reconnects the present with the past and the future. Here, they may discover new alliances and formations harnessed to the technologies of our time that will aid their drive for emancipation. Africans have adopted the digital revolution in communications faster and more creatively than any previous phase of the machine revolution. We lead the world in some respects.

Kenya launched the first large-scale experiment in mobile money, the M-Pesa, which now has more than 17 million accounts in that country. Because of the entrenched power of its banks and telecoms networks, South Africa has made halting progress in this revolution. In recent years, however, mobile money has taken off there as well, led by migrants from neighbouring countries such as Zimbabwe and thanks especially to a remarkably innovative finance act (the 2015 concessions to the Financial Intelligence Centre Act, No. 38 of 2001).

As a digital financial innovation linked to cellular phones, mobile money grants people greater freedom to manage their finances in a context of state monopoly currencies. Despite the influence of dominant financial institutions, it allows for a degree of self-determination and fosters economic pluralism. People are individuals who belong to society. We saw that mobile money emerged out of several alliances between grassroots initiatives and major corporations and bureaucracies. People themselves, however, did not launch the satellites that made this possible.

Lesotho's economy has developed beyond what it was in the nineteenth century, when cattle raiding, horses and guns shaped a temporary economic independence, and when it depended on miners' wages. The Basotho must selectively harness the benefits of these new digital technologies, since they can be adapted to, and shaped by, local conditions; this is how mobile money emerged in Kenya.

I hope that this book will play a small part in the renewal of interest in African economic history, which emerged in the mid-twentieth century in response to modernisation theory and imperial historiography (Green and Nyambara 2015; Austin and Broadberry 2014; Hopkins 2009, 2011, Austin 2008; Zeleza 1993). The discipline emerged in 'response to the colonial denigration of the African past and claims by colonialists that they had brought civilisation to the continent, which, hitherto, had neither history nor any achievements' (Mlambo 2018: 14).

Against the prevailing trend for economists and their public sponsors to separate economy from politics, my emphasis here has been on the political nature of all economies, including Lesotho's. Cliometrics – the reduction of economic history to numerical calculation – has its powerful adherents in our times. When globalisation fuelled by 'free trade' depends on soldiers to impose its methods on a small mountainous country in Africa, refusal to acknowledge the role of politics in economy serves only ruling interests.

This monograph does not tell one big story. I have asked a basic question: Why have the Basotho – a people who were able to stand up for themselves in their region during the mid-nineteenth century – struggled under such tyranny since then? The answers lie in the historical details and an eclectic approach to the schools of economic history currently available. The 'golden years' of Moshoeshoe's rule provide 'utopian resources' for Basotho that 'serve as a basis for a radical critique and remaking of the present'.[1] Various moments of victory during and after British rule perform a similar role, but our aspirations for progress as a people should draw on the historical substance of that earlier age of expansion for reinforcement.

NOTE

1. These words are adapted from a statement made by Achille Mbembe (2019) in reference to South Africa, in an interview with *Mail & Guardian*.

REFERENCES

Austin, G., and S. Broadberry. 2014. 'Introduction: The Renaissance of African Economic History', *Economic History Review* 67(4): 893–906.

Austin, G. 2008. 'The "Reversal of Fortune" Thesis and the Compression of History: Perspectives from African and Comparative Economic History', *Journal of International Development* 20(8): 996–1027.

Green, E., and Nyambara, P. 2015. 'The Internationalization of Economic History: Perspectives from the African Frontier', *Economic History of Developing Regions* 30(1): 68–78.

Hart, K. (ed.). 2015. *Economy For and Against Democracy*. New York: Berghahn Books.

———. (ed.). 2017. *Money in the Human Economy*. New York: Berghahn Books.

Hart, K., and J. Sharp (eds). 2014. *People, Money and Power in the Economic Crisis: Perspectives from the Global South*. Oxford: Berghahn Books.

Hart, K., J. Laville and A.D. Cattani. 2010. 'Building the Human Economy Together', in K. Hart, J. Laville and A.D. Cattani (eds), *The Human Economy: A Citizen's Guide*. Cambridge: Polity Press, pp. 1–17.

Hopkins, A.G. 2009. 'The New Economic History of Africa', *The Journal of African History* 50(2): 155–77.

Hopkins, A.G. 2011. 'Causes and Confusions in African History', *Economic History in Developing Regions* 26(2): 107–10.

Mlambo, A. 2018. 'African Economic History and Historiography', in T. Spear (ed.), The *Oxford Research Encyclopaedia of African History: Methods and Sources*. Oxford: Oxford University Press.

Mbembe, A. 2019. 'If We Don't Rehabilitate Reason, We Will Not Be Able to Fix Our Broken World', *Mail & Guardian*, 9 May 2019. Retrieved 16 December 2019 from https://mg.co.za/article/2019-05-09-if-we-dont-rehabilitate-reason-we-will-not-be-able-to-fix-our-broken-world.

Zeleza, P.T. 1993. *A Modern Economic History of Africa, Vol. 1: The Nineteenth Century*. Nairobi: East African Educational Publishers Ltd.

Index

www.ingramcontent.com/pod-product-compliance
Ingram Content Group UK Ltd.
Pitfield, Milton Keynes, MK11 3LW, UK
UKHW021839100926
8556IPUK00004B/439

9 781789 209815